JUDGMENT AT NUREMBERG

JUDGMENT AT NUREMBERG

BY **ABBY MANN**

A NEW DIRECTIONS BOOK

For inquiries regarding performance rights, please contact the author's agent,
Mr. Mitch Douglas, ICM, 40 West 57th Street, New York, NY 10019.

Book design by Sylvia Frezzolini Severance
Manufactured in the United States of America
New Directions Books are printed on acid-free paper.
First published as New Directions Paperbook 951 in 2002

Library of Congress Cataloging-in-Publication Data
Mann, Abby.
Judgment at Nuremberg / Abby Mann.
p. cm. — (New Directions paperbook ; 951)
ISBN 978-0-8112-1526-8 (alk. paper)
1. Nuremberg Trial of Major German War Criminals, Nuremberg,
Germany, 1945–1946—Drama. 2. Nuremberg (Germany)—Drama.
3. War crime trials—Drama. I. Title.
PS3563.A534 J83 2002
812'.54—dc21   2002006990

10 9 8 7 6

New Directions Books are published for James Laughlin
by New Directions Publishing Corporation
80 Eighth Avenue, New York 10011

TABLE OF CONTENTS

Introduction   vii

Cast of Characters   xxiii

Production Note   xxv

Judgment at Nuremberg   1

INTRODUCTION

O n March 26, 2001, the opening night of *Judgment at Nuremberg* on Broadway, I stood backstage at the Longacre Theatre. I knew the theater well. As a student at NYU, I used to sneak into second acts at theatres including the Longacre because I didn't have enough money to pay for a ticket and a good many times I would be humbled by ushers asking me to leave.

Anita Ross, the stage manager, pushed me toward the curtain. "Go!" I went on stage to take a curtain call with the illustrious cast. Looking out at the audience that included Walter Cronkite, Elie Wiesel, Sidney Poitier, Mario Cuomo and my closest friend, Tony Bennett, I thought of the events that had brought me here.

When I first began writing *Judgment at Nuremberg* in the fall of 1957, it was considered a breach of good manners to bring up the subject of German guilt for the events that happened during the Third Reich. There were even those who denied that a Holocaust had ever happened. There was a new crisis with the Russians and Germany was suddenly our ally. Therefore it was eagerly accepted that the German people had been hypnotized by a great orator, Hitler, and the camps were so removed from the German people that they had no inkling about some of the greatest crimes committed in our century or any century. There was no demand or even appetite for further explanation. Even from me though I had more reason than some to ask.

I grew up in East Pittsburgh, a suburb of Pittsburgh and the home of Westinghouse, a town populated by blue-collar workers employed by the company. My father, Ben Goodman, owned a one-man jewelry store. At high school there were students who would often taunt me because of my name, Abraham Goodman, and the fact that my dad spoke with an accent and we were middle class while they were struggling to survive. These taunts became even more disturbing when I listened to the short-wave broadcasts from Germany from people like Ezra Pound and a man with an American accent who called himself "Mr. O.K." and talked about how Jews were corrupting America and that soon he and the Nazis would be in New York to straighten things out.

Inducted into the Army when I was seventeen, I was sent to Fort Eustice where I found that I had not left East Pittsburgh behind me. Many of the men in my barracks shared the same prejudices and repeated the taunts for Abe Goodman. Tom Brokaw has said this was "the greatest generation," men who sacrificed their lives to defeat prejudice and save the world. There were, of course, those who understood and cared and did want to wipe out everything the Third Reich stood for. But the mundane truth was that the majority went because the government told them to go—the same way a later generation went to Vietnam. Since I was one of the worst privates in the United States Army, it was lucky for me that I developed pneumonia; while I was in the hospital, doctors found that my eyesight did not meet Army standards, so I was discharged. The irony did not escape me that men who had no basic feeling about the war were to die while I, who had some idea of what it was about, survived.

The first time I gave Nuremberg any real thought was when I met Abraham Pomerantz at a dinner party in New York in 1957. Pomerantz had been one of the prosecutors in the last trials at Nuremberg when the defendants included diplomats, doctors and judges. He had left when he found that most of the judges willing to serve at these trials were political hacks. Judges who could have made a real contribution did not go because Nuremberg had become unpopular and being part of it might hurt their careers. I was intrigued by what Pomerantz told me and he suggested I talk to Telford Taylor, who had been head of the prosecution at Nuremberg.

Taylor was a personable, articulate, courageous man who had left a promising career to go to Nuremberg. Later, he was to become one of the most eloquent and consistent voices against McCarthyism and Vietnam. He said the most significant of the trials was that of the judges in Germany. Why? Because these judges' minds had not been warped at an early age. Having reached maturity long before Hitler's rise to power, they embraced the ideologies of the Third Reich as educated adults. "They, most of all," Taylor said, "should have valued justice."

Intrigued, I read through the transcripts of the Justice Trials. Appearing before the judges to have their fates decided: a man sterilized because of his political beliefs; a woman sent to prison for having a relationship with an older Jewish man, though it was never proven that they were sexually intimate—just the fact that they were friends was enough to send the Jewish man to his death and to send her to jail for years, ostensibly for perjury.

In the German judges' final statements some were unrepentant. One said, "Your Honors, the highest thing a man can do is do his duty to his country. I upheld my oath of allegiance to my fatherland and to its laws. As a judge, I could do no other. I believe Your Honors will find me, and millions of Germans like me, to be not guilty."

There was, however, a defendant whose justification for joining the Third Reich had alarming overtones. In effect, it was this: "The country is in danger. What difference does it make if a few political extremists lose their rights? What difference does it make if a few racial minorities lose their rights? It is only a passing phase. It is only a stage we are going through. It will be discarded sooner or later. And then one day, we looked around and found we were in even more terrible danger. The rites began in this courtroom, swept over our land like a raging, roaring disease! What was going to be a passing phase had become a way of life."

McCarthyism was at its height when I read these transcripts. While there were no gas chambers, people were being destroyed financially and jailed because of their political beliefs or even because of who they knew. The question was on the table: Could what happened in Germany happen elsewhere?

I had been working in Los Angeles on a screenplay for Paramount, but the transcripts haunted me. I talked on the phone to Herbert Brodkin, one of the producers of the TV program *Playhouse 90*. He was interested. I left Hollywood and went back to New York. I was giving up a thousand-dollar-a-week job for a five-hundred-dollar advance.

I went to Germany and I met some of the participants in the Nazi regime. Leni Riefenstahl was one. She had done the infamous film which helped so much to promote Hitler, *Triumph of the Will*. She suggested we meet in the cellar of her apartment building, where she had set up a projector. She wanted to show me the last film she had been working on. When I questioned her about the camps and what had happened, she said, of course, she knew very little about it. She didn't think that even Hitler really knew. It was Goebbels and Himmler and the others. I questioned her about Hitler. She said he was terrible yet wonderful in many ways. There was something electric about him. She had gone, with her husband, to see him in the last days in his bunker. And she wanted me to know that if he had asked her, she would have stayed and died with him.

I talked to one of the industrialists who had been a defendant in the first trial at Nuremberg and was acquitted. While he had been repentant at the trial, he was not repentant now. All during the conversation, he spoke only in German. Only at the end he spoke in perfect English to say, "Be careful you don't have an accident while you are in Germany." I turned and said to him, "If I have an accident, you'll have an accident." I left the house feeling brave. Then I jumped at something I saw. It turned out to be my own shadow.

The most poignant meeting that I had was with the widow of a general who had been convicted at Nuremberg. It was in her apartment in Munich. She had a large portrait of her husband on the wall. She told me that she and her husband hated Hitler. That he had been placed on trial with the Nazi political leaders and was made to seem one of them. He was part of the revenge the victors always take on the vanquished. She told me about the cruelty of the authorities at Nuremberg. Her husband had been a military man all his life. He was entitled to a soldier's death. She went from official to official asking that he be permitted the dignity of a firing squad. But he was hanged with the others. She told me that after that she knew what it meant to hate. She told me that for a long while she had never left the house. Never left her room. Drank. She hated with every fiber of her being. She hated every American she had ever known. But she discovered one can't live with hate. She said, "We have to forget. We have to forget if we are to go on living." She wanted the whole world to know that. She was writing her memoirs. But somehow she was unable to finish. I thought I knew why. There were things she couldn't bear to face. Yet was there not truth in what she was saying? Wouldn't it be better to forget?

Most importantly of all, I went to see Robert Kempner in Locarno, Switzerland. Robert Kempner was one of the most illustrious lawyers in Germany during the pre-Nazi era. As a matter of fact, he prosecuted Hitler when he was arrested because of his actions in a beer hall *putsch* to overthrow the government. Things Kempner told me were illuminating. He said the myth that Hitler was a great orator was garbage. In his own words, he said, "He was a noisy, vulgar fellow. They sentenced him to six years but he complained so loudly they let him out in five months." What did he have, I wanted to know, that made the German people follow him? "They didn't follow him anywhere they didn't want to go. He knew the German people. He knew what they wanted. And he gave it to them.

The myth is that he succeeded in spite of anti-Semitism. The truth is he succeeded because of it." I talked to Kempner about my project and what the General's wife had told me: "We must forget. We must forget if we are to go on living." Kempner said, "You know what's wrong with that? Then all these people would have died for no reason and no one was responsible and it will happen again."

I finished the script. I tried to the best of my ability to find the most powerful thing one could learn from the greatest crimes in recorded history. It is spoken by Judge Haywood, the central character of the play. It is this:

> *This trial has shown that under the stress of a national crisis, ordinary men, even able and extraordinary men, can delude themselves into the commission of crimes and atrocities so vast and heinous as to stagger the imagination. No one who has sat through this trial can ever forget. The sterilization of men because of their political beliefs . . . The murder of children . . . How easily it can happen. There are those in our country today, too, who speak of the protection of the country. Of survival. The answer to that is: survival as what? A country isn't a rock. And it isn't an extension of one's self. It's what it stands for, when standing for something is the most difficult.*

Before we could get into rehearsal, people in the Eisenhower administration had read the script and said it would hurt our efforts to get the German people on our side in the struggle with the Russians. They persuaded CBS to cancel it. I called our producer Brodkin. He said that one thing was certain: *Judgment at Nuremberg* would not be done. But the script had

an advocate who was not willing to let it rest: George Roy
Hill, a brilliant director who was later to do *Butch Cassidy and
the Sundance Kid* and *The Sting*.

There were meetings with Hill and the cast. I believe it was
Hill who suggested that we take a full page ad out in *The New
York Times* saying that it was important that the American people see this production. I began composing the ad when CBS
decided with the controversy building that it was the better
part of valor to go ahead with the production.

Rehearsals began. For the first time in my life—and the last
time—I had no notes for the actors or the director. We gathered a cast that was remarkable under any circumstances, and
particularly one for television: Claude Rains, Melvyn Douglas,
Paul Lukas and a young German actor, Maximilian Schell.

I watched the live broadcast from my apartment. It was a
wonderful production. At one point, Claude Rains broke
down at the emotion of what he was feeling about the events
that had passed. At the end of it I said to myself, "Well, now let's
see what the American people think about that."

But then once again something happened. One of the
sponsors, American Gas, Inc., had sent a memo demanding that
we delete any mention of gas. They didn't want to be held
responsible for what happened in the Holocaust under any circumstances. Hill and the cast refused, so that when the climac-
tic moment came in the production when Judge Haywood as
played by Claude Rains says to Paul Lukas, the German judge,
"I understand the pressures that you faced. No man can say how
he would have faced those pressures himself unless he had actually been tested. But how can you expect me to forgive sending millions of people to gas ovens?" American Gas took mat-

ters into their own hands: they had an executive at CBS pump out the words "gas ovens" so that Claude Rains mouthed the words but no sound came out.

This incident overshadowed, as far as the media was concerned, anything else about the production. The pumping out of the word "gas." That was what was important. Not German guilt. Not our own lack of responsibility or that millions of people were killed without reason. Censorship was what was important. People who watched the television show didn't feel that way. A record number of calls for a dramatic program flooded the network. However, the Emmys reacted the way they usually do to the evaluation of the media. We were passed by. We didn't receive one nomination.

I tried to sell it as a film, but the studios could not be less interested. They said, "You made your point."

I tried to put *Judgment at Nuremberg* out of my mind. I showed a copy of another television drama I had written, *A Child Is Waiting*, to the wonderful Katharine Hepburn. It was the first drama to deal with retarded children. Hepburn wanted to do it if we could obtain the right director. I went to Europe to talk to Jack Clayton and Jules Dassin when my agent called me with the incredible news that Hepburn had shown a copy of *Judgment at Nuremberg* to Spencer Tracy and he wanted to do the role of Judge Haywood. My thoughts went back to the time I was writing *Judgment at Nuremberg* in my one-room apartment in New York. I had dreamed of one actor doing it. That actor was Tracy. He was the essence of America, all that was good about it in one man.

Tracy wanted the remarkable Stanley Kramer to produce

and direct it. Kramer had such admiration for Tracy that he would have done almost anything that Tracy suggested. So it really was Tracy that was responsible for the film being done.

I'll always remember the first reading of the screenplay, because surrounding me were the figures who were the very essence of motion pictures and whose legends have grown through the years. Besides Tracy, there were Marlene Dietrich playing the general's widow, Burt Lancaster, Judy Garland, Montgomery Clift, Richard Widmark, and the young actor that had performed so brilliantly in the television production, Maximilian Schell. After the reading Tracy said, "Let's get one thing straight. The role that's going to win an Academy Award is the one that Max is playing. I'm just doing it because I want it done."

It was United Artists' crazy idea to open the film in Berlin. On the plane going over was not only Judy Garland but a group of reporters, including Max Lerner, who was considered a great "liberal," but who strongly objected to the film. He said it would hurt our country, "It's going to embarrass the Eisenhower administration." Judy answered him saying, "If that administration could be embarrassed, it would have dropped dead a long time ago."

When we reached Berlin, there were reports that there might be violent protests. I went up to the suite in the hotel where Spence was staying. He was not well but he had insisted on coming to Germany for the opening. I talked to him about the threats and suggested that perhaps he shouldn't come that night. Tracy said, "I'm going."

Tracy and I started to walk from our hotel to the Congress Halle, where the film was going to be shown for the first time.

Tracy said with his acerbic humor, "I hope we get out of this alive." All of a sudden we heard a wild, hysterical yell. Someone grabbed Tracy from behind. Tracy was too frightened to look around and see who it was. The two of them continued to walk for a moment with the figure behind Tracy still holding onto him with what seemed to be a strangle hold. The figure turned out to be Montgomery Clift, who had been drinking and was expressing his affection for his idol.

After the film was shown, there was dead silence in the audience. Even Willy Brandt, one of the most literate and sensitive leaders in Europe, hedged his bets. He thanked everyone for coming and said he would have to study this document to see what he would have to say about it.

There was a deadly pall at the festive dinner that had been arranged for after the showing. A press conference followed. A woman got up and said to Tracy, "You know, Mr. Tracy, the German people love you perhaps more than any other American actor. We find it hard to believe that you would appear in such a harsh movie about our people. We read in an interview where you said, in reply to some movies you were doing, that you did them for the money. Is that why you did this one? You don't really believe what this movie says, do you?" Tracy put his tongue in his cheek, in extraordinary Tracy fashion, and said, "Every word."

Judy and I decided we would stay over a couple of days just to see what was happening in the theaters with *Nuremberg* before going to New York for the opening there. After the showing, we came upon a young man who was saying to whoever would listen that it was a disgrace to show the film in Berlin. It turned out that he was the son of one of the judges portrayed in the film. I tried to talk with him. One of the publicity guys from United Artists started to get skittish and said, "I think we'd better go, Mr. Mann." The German judge's son turned to me and said, "Are you Abby Mann?" I was silent. "You wrote this?" He advanced toward me and spoke to me half in German and half in English. I tried to put things into perspective. Judy Garland kept tugging me and said, "Let's go." A crowd gathered around us. There were ominous sounds from the people surrounding us that I didn't understand, having no knowledge of German. Police entered the lobby. The publicity guy from United Artists had thought it was best to bring them in. They escorted us out swiftly.

The fate of *Judgment at Nuremberg* as a motion picture was far different than how it had been received on television. Max and I won the New York Film Critics Award. Then the film was nominated for twelve Academy Awards. Max won for Best Actor and I won for Best Screenplay. But the award I prize most was not from the Academy. It was in a wire I received from Tracy in which he said, "All I can say is if the lights go out now I still win. Please do not forget it was a great privilege to say those words. Love, Spence."

In the following years, to quote Colonel Lawson in the fim, "mankind has not crossed over Jordan." There was Rwanda. There was Bosnia and Milosovic. Genocide was not dead. As a result, the United Nations created an International Criminal Court for bringing to justice perpetrators of genocide, war crimes, and crimes against humanity. One hundred thirty countries joined the Court but not the United States.

On January 1, 2001, President Clinton signed the treaty for

the entrance of the United States into the Court. He said, "In taking this action, we join more than 130 other countries to reaffirm our strong support for international accountability. The United States has a history of commitment to this principle based on our involvement in the Nuremberg Tribunals."

Senator Jesse Helms of North Carolina called Mr. Clinton's decision "as outrageous as it is inexplicable. I have a message for the outgoing President. This decision will not stand." The new President, George W. Bush, withdrew the United States from the International Criminal Court. The reason given was that if there should be such a court it could inhibit the ability of the United States to use its military to meet alliance obligations. Were they thinking of Grenada and Panama? Were they afraid that one day members of our own government might be defendants? Unfortunately, *Judgment at Nuremberg* seemed to be more timely than ever.

I got a call from Fred Walker and Tony Randall, the Managing Director and Founder of National Actors Theatre. They wanted to do *Judgment at Nuremberg* as a play on Broadway. Their attempt to make a permanent American repertory company comparable to those that existed in London was something I responded to. I told them I'd do it on one condition: that Max Schell, who had been responsible for so much of the success of the previous productions, be part of it.

I had dinner with Schell. He wanted to do it. But he asked to play the main defendant, the role that Paul Lukas and Burt Lancaster had played, not the defense attorney, the role for which he had won an Academy Award.

We were able to recruit a cast who were not only enormously talented but cared deeply about the play and what it says. Besides Schell there were Tony Award winner George Grizzard, Marthe Keller, who had made such an impression in *Black Sunday* and *Marathon Man*, Joe Wiseman, now in his eighties, who was so marvelous in *Detective Story* and *Viva Zapata*, and Michael Hayden in the Max Schell role. Hayden was the one who redefined *Carousel* with his portrayal of Billy Bigelow. Suddenly it was uncertain whether we would get Schell. He was ill. It was feared it might be fatal. But he recovered and I will always be grateful for his appearance. As much as I liked Lancaster in the film, Max added a dimension that had not been there before. He seemed to bring Germany right onto the stage. He made the tragedy all the more human and authentic.

The audiences were moved by the play even more, it seemed to me, than they were by the film. Maybe part of it was that it took time for the events to seem real. Maybe it was also because we were sharing a live moment together which something on film can never do.

Then, shortly after the play closed, we experienced something that had not happened since 1812. Our country was attacked. The Twin Towers were destroyed and thousands of people were murdered. The television company Al-Jazeera encouraged rumors that the attacks on the towers had been done by the Israeli Moussad to instigate a war against those of the Muslim faith. It was no surprise that this was taken as gospel in Muslim Arab countries. Pick up a newspaper in any part of the Arab world and you could see a swastika superimposed on the Israeli flag. But what happened next was a surprise. Bin Laden appeared on videotape and proclaimed the attack had been done because of the United States' support of Israel and to protest the oppression of the Palestinian people. Bin Laden had never done anything to help the Palestinians or even expressed sympathy for them. Yet many intellectuals in Europe did not dismiss this out of hand. Some of them even intimated that the destruction of the towers might have been somewhat justified. For nearly a decade anti-Semitic violence in France had been rare. But after the bin Laden appearance, it was no longer rare. Members of a Jewish soccer team in France were attacked by a gang of hooded youths shouting "Death to Jews!" wielding metal sticks and bars. A synagogue in Marseille was destroyed by arson and another in nearby Belgium was damaged when five firebombs were thrown inside. In Moscow anti-Semitic slogans were spray-painted over a mural of Nobel Laureate Andrei Sakharov. In Germany—Germany!—three synagogues were set on fire over the Passover-Easter weekend. A swastika was painted on a memorial to Jewish victims of Nazism in Berlin. Right-wing parties with anti-Semitic platforms were coming into power. Why? Why was it happening now? Was this feeling lurking all this time and seeking a moment to justify itself? Was it now because they could say here was the proof they were looking for that something was wrong with the Jews after all? Were they trying to find a way to get themselves off the hook for what they had done and what they did not do during the Holocaust?

It was almost as though the Holocaust never happened and the Nuremberg trials never took place.

And then I remembered a talk I had with Martin Luther King while I was writing a film about his life. He said to me that the Holocaust was the only event in his life that made him wonder whether there was an Almighty. If there were, how could He have let this happen? I replied, "Maybe the murders of millions including women and children showed where hate can lead and it will be a deterrent for anything like it to ever happen again." King smiled. In that weary smile was a lifetime of having to deal with people who would not give up their hate and who needed someone they could strike out at and punish for the tragedy of their lives. After all, it absolved them and their leaders of any responsibility for their predicament and any need for self-examination. In King's smile also was the observation that I didn't know much about human nature.

ABBY MANN
August 2002

CAST OF CHARACTERS

Judgment at Nuremberg premiered at the Longacre Theatre, New York City, on March 26, 2001, produced by the National Actors Theatre, Tony Randall, Artistic Director, in association with Earle I. Mack. It was directed by John Tillinger; set design by James Noone; costume design by Jess Goldstein; lighting design by Brian MacDevitt; original music and sound by David Van Tieghem; and projections by Elaine J. McCarthy. The cast, in order of appearance, was as follows:

NARRATOR	Philip Lestrange
COLONEL PARKER	Robert Foxworth
JUDGE HAYWOOD	George Grizzard
GENERAL MERRIN	Jack Davidson
CAPTAIN BYERS	Peter Francis James
COURT INTERPRETER 1	Peter Hermann
EMIL HAHN	Peter Maloney
COURT INTERPRETER 2	Jurian Hughes
FREDERICK HOFFSTETTER	Philip Lestrange
WERNER LAMMPE	Reno Roop
OSKAR ROLFE	Michael Hayden
ERNST JANNING	Maximilian Schell
JUDGE NORRIS	Henry Strozier
JUDGE IVES	Fred Burrell

GUARD	Ty Jones
DR. WICKERT	Joseph Wiseman
MRS. HALBESTADT	Patricia Conolly
FRAU BERTHOLT	Marthe Keller
RUDOLPH PETERSON	Michael Mastro
GEUTER★	Peter Kybart
MARIA WALLNER	Heather Randall
THEA★	Kellie Overbey
WAITER★	Peter Hermann
ELSA LINDNOW★	Susan Kellermann

★ These characters were used in the Broadway production but are optional at the discretion of the director.

A German language production of *Judgment at Nuremberg* opened October 22, 2002 at the Stadtische Buhnen Theatre in Nuremberg, Germany, directed by Klaus Kusenberg. *Judgment at Nuremberg* will also be staged in German at the Ernst-Deutsch-Theatre in Hamburg Germany in February 2003, directed by Johannes Kaetzler, as well as in Japanese at the Shin Kobe Oriental Theatre in the City of Kobe, Japan, and the Kinokuniya Southern Theatre in Tokyo, Japan, both in 2003.

Act I and Act II:
Nuremberg, Germany — 1947

PRODUCTION NOTE

In our production of *Judgment at Nuremberg* at the Longacre Theatre in New York, we used only one substantial set: the courtroom. The rest of the locales were done with a minimal suggestion of sets. The projections and/or slides are optional.

A.M.

for Myra

JUDGMENT AT
NUREMBERG

PROLOGUE

NARRATOR: On January 1, 2001, then President Clinton signed the Rome Treaty for an International Criminal Court. He said, "In taking this action, we reaffirm our support for international accountability and for bringing to justice perpetrators of genocide, war crimes, crimes against humanity based on our involvement in the Nuremberg Tribunals that brought Nazi war criminals to justice." Senator Jesse Helms of North Carolina called Mr. Clinton's decision "as outrageous as it is inexplicable. I have a message for the outgoing President. This decision will not stand." Many others echoed Senator Helms' objections, including the incoming President Bush. Their reason was it could inhibit the ability of the United States to use its military to meet alliance obligations and participate in multinational operations.

[*U.S. Army news reel footage of the first Nuremberg Trials in 1946 is shown.*]

NARRATOR: The first of the Nuremberg trials were concluded on October 1, 1946.
"Herman Goering, Reichsmarshall. Charged with conspiracy, crimes against peace, war crimes, crimes against humanity. The verdict: guilty on all accounts. The sentence: death by hanging."

"Rudolph Hess, Deputy Führer. Verdict: guilty on two counts. Sentence: life imprisonment.

"Joachim von Ribbentrop, Reich Minister for Foreign Affairs. Verdict: guilty on all counts. Sentence: death by hanging."

Nuremberg, Germany. October 1, 1946. The conclusion of the trial of twenty-two top Nazis accused of war crimes. Twelve were sentenced to death. Three were acquitted. Seven received prison sentences ranging from ten years to life.

October 16, 1946. The sentences of death were carried out. Julius Streicher. Von Ribbentrop. Wilhelm Keitel. Ernst Kaltenbrunner. All except Herman Goering who cheated the hangman by taking his own life.

The first of the Nuremberg trials were over. Still to come were twelve more trials of 177 diplomats, generals, SS officers, high Nazi officials, doctors, judges, directors of IG Farben, and leading German business and professional men, whose cooperation was essential to the success of the Nazi conspiracy.

ACT ONE

SCENE: NUREMBERG. PALACE OF JUSTICE—
CORRIDOR—TWO YEARS LATER

[*Colonel Tad Parker walks down the corridor with General Matthew Merrin. Parker is the head of the prosecution of the remaining Nuremberg trials. It is not difficult to see why he has been spoken of as a man with a political future. He has at his fingertips a complete command of the legal procedure, and a hard-hitting, precise sense of delivery. Add to this an erect, handsome presence. Yet there is something else beneath the surface of the man. A weariness. A weariness akin to sickness. He has looked into a great deal of evil in man. It has affected him. It has robbed him of a basic buoyancy and optimism.*

General Merrin, a vigorous man in his fifties, is personable, intelligent. He sees his job through one lens: is it good for his country?

Captain Byers enters with Judge Dan Haywood. Haywood is the "vanishing American." He is like many men in his fifties trying to find his identity. A man with far greater capacities than he realizes. Earl Warren was thought by many to be a professional party hack until he was on the Supreme Court. Haywood is such a man, also.

Captain Byers is a black man in his late twenties. He is graduated from West Point.]

COLONEL PARKER: Hello Judge.

HAYWOOD: Hello.

CAPT. BYERS: This is General Merrin.

HAYWOOD: Hello.

GENERAL MERRIN: Ever been to Germany before?

HAYWOOD: Just once. In World War I.

COLONEL PARKER: Your quarters okay?

HAYWOOD: They've given me this mansion with three servants and this garden. I got lost trying to find my way to the
bedroom. I really don't need all this.

COLONEL PARKER: When the government does something
it does it right. You know that.

HAYWOOD: Three servants?

CAPT. BYERS: We're doing it for them as well as for you.
This way they eat.

HAYWOOD: I guess I need three servants.

COLONEL PARKER: Good to have you here. We need people like you.

HAYWOOD: I'm sure I was the only man in America qualified for the job.

COLONEL PARKER: I beg your pardon?

HAYWOOD: There have been trials of Goering. Streicher. Frank. A lot of people think it's enough.

COLONEL PARKER [*dryly*]: So?

HAYWOOD: So it's made a hell of a lack of candidates for this job. You even had to beat the backwoods of North Carolina to come up with a hick like me.

[*Pause.*]

COLONEL PARKER: I hope you're not sorry you came.

HAYWOOD: No. I'm not sorry I came. I just want you to know I know where the bodies are buried. The only thing is I don't know anything about international law.

COLONEL PARKER: Who does? Except a few professors at Columbia—and I'm not sure they know.

HAYWOOD: I hope I'm up to it.

COLONEL PARKER: Of course you are. Relax. Enjoy things while you can. I'm sure you'll get used to living in a big house and having three servants. Capt. Byers, show Judge Haywood around Nuremberg. It's a fascinating place. Goes back to 1219. Enjoy the lakes and the greenery. They have no politics.

HAYWOOD: I would like to see something of the town, something of the people.

CAPT. BYERS: Nuremberg is yours Sir, what there is left of it.

[*Haywood and Captain Byers exit. Colonel Parker looks at General Merrin bitterly.*]

COLONEL PARKER: He's right. He's not up to it. [*Bitterly.*] My God. The way we started. We had men like Biddle and Jackson. Now we have hicks from the hinterlands with plenty of experience in traffic violations.

SCENE: KAROLINA STRASSE, NUREMBERG

[*Capt. Byers leads Haywood down what was once the center of Nuremberg's business section.*]

CAPT. BYERS: This is the main street. It's called Karolina Strasse, Sir.

HAYWOOD: You're career Army, aren't you, Captain?

CAPT. BYERS: Yes Sir.

HAYWOOD: What's your first name?

CAPT. BYERS: Harrison. Harry.

HAYWOOD: Well, Harry, you see I'm not Army and this formality makes me a little uncomfortable. Do you think it would be too much an infraction of rules for you to call me "Judge" or "Dan" or something?

CAPT. BYERS: Yes Sir—Judge.

HAYWOOD: How long have you been here Harry?

CAPT. BYERS: Two years.

HAYWOOD: Two years. It's a long time.

CAPT. BYERS: Yes Sir, judge.

HAYWOOD: Have any friends here?

CAPT. BYERS: Sure.

HAYWOOD: German friends?

CAPT. BYERS: They're too friendly to be friends.

HAYWOOD: A girl?

CAPT. BYERS: Yes. Her parents were Nazis. But she was eight years old when they came to power.

HAYWOOD: I didn't ask that.

CAPT. BYERS: I know, but maybe you were thinking it. It's natural to think about it. I thought if anybody was going to indoctrinate her it might as well be me.

[*Both laugh.*]

HAYWOOD: You don't care much for this assignment do you?

CAPT. BYERS: Not much.

HAYWOOD: Don't you think the trials are important?

CAPT. BYERS: My feelings are the same as Churchill's. We should have held a military trial and shot them.

HAYWOOD: If they were found guilty.

CAPT. BYERS: After they were found guilty. Then we can start getting ready for the next war.

HAYWOOD: And what war might that be?

CAPT. BYERS: The war with the Russians, of course.

HAYWOOD: I see.

CAPT. BYERS: Well, you're in the heart of what used to be Nuremberg's business section. You know, Nuremberg was a great toy center.

HAYWOOD: Really?

CAPT. BYERS: It was also the anti-Semitism center. This is where the first authorized violence against the Jews happened.

HAYWOOD: Authorized?

CAPT. BYERS: Hitler and his government tried an experiment. They decided on a 24-hour boycott of Jewish stores. They wanted to see whether the average German would protest or if they would be taken to task by the newspapers and the radio programs. It was a great success, better than they ever dreamed. The SS painted the shop windows and made the Jewish proprietors come out and clean the sidewalks—with a toothbrush no less.

[*Capt. Byers continues to explain what happened. As he does, we see on the screen behind them documentary footage of Crystal Night. Jewish stars painted on store windows. Proprietors being beaten in the streets. A woman being pulled through the street by her hair by German soldiers. After the footage has faded, there is a moment of silence.*]

HAYWOOD: Hard to believe it really happened, isn't it?

CAPT. BYERS: Not for me.

HAYWOOD: Why?

CAPT. BYERS [*looks at couple passing by*]: I've known these people. They speak another language and dress differently, but they're just like people in my hometown, people in my own unit.

HAYWOOD: What are you trying to say? Are you trying to say what happened here could happen at home?

CAPT. BYERS: Can I imagine that the people there would have done things like this if there wasn't a government to stop them and they might be punished? I guess a day doesn't pass when I don't wonder about that. [*Pause; he sees that Haywood is disturbed.*] Sorry if I've upset you. But people with my shade of skin react differently to what happened here than people with your shade of skin.

HAYWOOD: I understand.

CAPT. BYERS: Come on. I'll take you to Zeppelin Field where they held the rallies.

SCENE: PALACE OF JUSTICE—COURTROOM

[*Haywood and two other judges, Ives and Norris, enter. They sit before their individual microphones. Ives is in his sixties. He has been at Nuremberg since the trials started. He is a political conservative and he has found himself surprisingly identifying with some of the men in the dock. Norris is in his late forties. A soft-spoken man with a New England accent. His main experience had been as a law professor in Maine. Like Haywood, he is awed by the position of responsibility he has been put in. The defendants are in their places in the dock. Colonel Parker and defense attorneys are present.*]

CAPT. BYERS: The Tribunal is now in session. God save the United States of America and this honorable Tribunal.

[*All are seated.*]

HAYWOOD: The Tribunal will arraign the defendants. The microphone will now be placed in front of the defendant Emil Hahn.

[*Erect, Hahn stares out at the Tribunal as though he were the accuser instead of the accused. His bald, alert head takes in every detail of the courtroom.*]

HAYWOOD: Emil Hahn. Are you represented by counsel before this Tribunal?

EMIL HAHN [*rises abruptly*]: Not guilty.

[*Pause.*]

HAYWOOD: The question is, are you represented by counsel before this Tribunal?

HAHN [*abruptly*]: I am represented.

HAYWOOD: How do you plead to the charges and specifications set forth in the indictment against you—guilty or not guilty?

HAHN: Not guilty on all counts.

HAYWOOD: You may be seated.

[*The microphone is placed before the next defendant. Hoffstetter is in his late forties. He wears a pince-nez. His clothing is correct and neat, making him look like nothing so much as a middle-class businessman who has fallen on hard times.*]

HAYWOOD: Frederick Hoffstetter. Are you represented by counsel before this Tribunal?

[*Hoffstetter looks at Haywood anxiously. His manner is courteous, straightforward and sincere.*]

HOFFSTETTER: Yes, Your Honor. I am represented by counsel.

HAYWOOD: How do you plead to the charges and specifications set forth in the indictment against you—guilty or not guilty?

HOFFSTETTER: Not guilty, Your Honor.

HAYWOOD: You may be seated.

[*Hoffstetter is seated. The microphone is placed before the next man. Werner Lammpe looks dully ahead, neither to the right nor the left. He is in his eighties. Everything seems a nightmare to him in these days. He is mystified at why he is here.*]

HAYWOOD: Werner Lammpe. Are you represented by counsel before this Tribunal?

LAMMPE [*his voice quavers tremulously*]: Counsel? Yes.

HAYWOOD: How do you plead to the charges and specifications set forth in the indictment against you—guilty or not guilty?

LAMMPE [*nods slowly, then looks toward Haywood; his lips tremble*]: Not guilty.

HAYWOOD: You may be seated.

[*Lammpe sits down. Microphone is placed before Ernst Janning, known as one of the great figures in the German judicial system in the pre-Nazi era. His every feature and characteristic is known to the German people. His enormous height, his stooped, hulking shoulders. Janning had been Minister of Justice of Germany and his reputation before that had been such that even Hitler tempered his antagonism toward him. Janning's defection to the Nazis is one of the most discussed mysteries of the era.*]

HAYWOOD: Ernst Janning, are you represented by counsel before this Tribunal?

[*Janning remains seated. The expression on his face is beyond that of not having heard what Haywood has said. Beyond that of not having any interest in what he has said.*]

HAYWOOD: Ernst Janning, are you represented by counsel before this Tribunal?

[*Oskar Rolfe, defense attorney for Janning, rises. He is in his early thirties. His training was mainly at the university of Berlin. He was unable to practice law because of the war. It had taken care of all that. Five bloody years ripped out of his life. He has sat in the Nuremberg courtroom for the last year and a half knowing this was the place to make up for them. He has watched Goering outwit a great American jurist, Robert Jackson. He has watched his own colleagues flounder and fall into irrelevancies and be lost in their own need for personal rationalizations. He has watched what he thought was a band of hypocrites justifying their own need for vengeance by high sounding verbiage covered over by moral platitudes that stood just so much scrutiny and no more. He is determined to take on these Americans and their concept of justice according to their own rules. He is determined to hoist them up by their own petards once and for all.*]

ROLFE: I represent the defendant Your Honors.

HAYWOOD [*still addressing Janning*]: How do you plead to the charges and specifications set forth in the indictment against you—guilty or not guilty?

[*The M.P. behind Janning brusquely raises him to his feet and snaps the earphones over his ears.*]

ROLFE: May I address the court.

HAYWOOD: Yes.

ROLFE: The defendant does not recognize the authority of this Tribunal and wishes to lodge a formal protest in lieu of pleading.

HAYWOOD: A plea of not guilty will be entered. The prosecution will make its opening statement.

COLONEL PARKER: Yes, Your Honor.

[*As he proceeds, Colonel Parker takes his place before the judges. He tries to restrain himself from expressing the emotion he feels about the defendants before him.*]

Your Honor, the case is unusual in that the defendants are charged with crimes committed in the name of the law. These men, together with their deceased or fugitive colleagues, are the embodiment of what passed for justice in the Third Reich. As judges on the bench you will be sitting in judgment of judges in the dock. This is as it should be. For only a judge knows how much more a court is than a courtroom. It is a process and a spirit. It is the House of Law. The defendants knew this too. They knew courtrooms well. They sat in their black robes. [*Emotion overcoming him.*] And they distorted and they perverted and they destroyed justice and law in Germany. They are, perhaps more than others, guilty of complicity in murders, tortures, atrocities—the most cruel and devastating this world has ever seen. Their minds were not warped at an early age. They had attained maturity long before Hitler's rise to power. They embraced the ideologies of the Third Reich as educated adults. They, most of all, should have valued justice. Here they will receive the justice they denied others. They will be judged according to the evidence presented in this courtroom. The prosecution asks nothing more. [*Returns to his desk.*]

HAYWOOD: Herr Rolfe will make the opening statement for the defense.

[*Rolfe rises slowly and goes before the Tribunal.*]

ROLFE: May it please the Tribunal. It is not only a great honor but also a great challenge for an advocate to aid this Tribunal in its task. The avowed purpose of this Tribunal is to find a code of justice the whole world will be responsible to. How will this code be established? It will be established in a clear, honest evaluation of the responsibility for the crimes in the indictment stated by the prosecution. In the words of the great American jurist, Oliver Wendell Holmes, "This responsibility will not be found only in documents. It will be found in consideration of a political or social nature. It will be found, most of all, in the character of men." [*Pause.*] What is the character of Ernst Janning? Let us examine his life for a moment. Following World War One, he became one of the leaders of the Weimar Republic and was one of the framers of its democratic constitution. He became Minister of Justice in Germany in 1935. A position the equivalent of the Attorney General of the United States. Finally, in a Reichstag speech of 26 April 1942, Hitler attacked Janning and forced him to resign. [*Pause.*] If Ernst Janning is to be found guilty, certain implications must arise. A judge does not make the law. He carries out the laws of his country, be it a democracy or a dictatorship. The statement, "My country right or wrong," was expressed by a great American patriot. It is no less true for a German patriot. Should Ernst Janning have carried out the laws of his country? Or should he have refused to carry them out and become a traitor? The defense is dedicated to finding responsibility as is the prosecution. For it is not only Ernst Janning who is on trial here. It is the German people.

SCENE: PALACE OF JUSTICE—JUDGES' CHAMBERS

[*Haywood, Ives and Norris enter.*]

HAYWOOD: Shakes you up a bit, doesn't it? These men were judges just like we are. And now they're sitting as defendants accused of crimes.

IVES: We'll see if they're criminals or not.

NORRIS: What do you mean?

IVES: When you've been here a while, you see it's not so cut and dried.

HAYWOOD: Hahn looks at us as though we're the criminals.

NORRIS: Lammpe doesn't seem to know what's going on.

IVES: Janning does. He refuses to acknowledge the authority of this court. And a lot of people think he's right.

HAYWOOD: I got hold of some of the books of Ernst Janning.

NORRIS: Are they translated into English?

HAYWOOD: Into a lot of languages. His textbooks are still used in universities all over the world. I had no idea how important he was until I got hold of this.

NORRIS [*taking the book*]: *The Profession of Law* by Ernst Janning. Is it interesting?

HAYWOOD: They are more than that; they're really a picture of an era in Germany, its hopes, its aspirations. They weren't so different from ours really.

IVES: A lot of people are upset about him being a part of all this.

HAYWOOD: Now, listen to this. On the signing of the Weimar constitution he wrote: "Now we can look forward to a Germany without guns and bloodshed. A Germany of justice where men can live instead of die. A Germany of purpose, of freedom, of humanity. A Germany that calls for the best in men." How could a man who wrote words like these be part of sterilizations and murders? How could he be?

NORRIS: Parker says he was.

HAYWOOD: I know. But the prosecution is going to have to prove every inch of its allegation against Janning. And to tell you the truth, I'm very uneasy sitting in judgment on a man of his stature.

IVES: Well, that's why we're here. We'll be talking about this until the end of the trial. Now, what are you fellows up to this weekend? My wife is planning a little get-together at the Grand Hotel Saturday night.

NORRIS: My wife and I are going to Liege.

IVES: There's nothing in Liege. I've been there.

NORRIS: My son was in the 101st. He is buried in the American cemetery outside Liege.

IVES: I am so sorry.

NORRIS: That's all right.

IVES: You'll come won't you, Dan?

HAYWOOD: Sure.

IVES: My wife was thinking she might bring someone along. Perhaps one of the women who work here at the Tribunal. She was concerned you might be lonely. We know you lost your wife recently.

HAYWOOD: I don't think I'm up to it right now, Curtiss. Maybe some time later.

IVES: Just let us know. [Pause.] I've got to get back. We have a dinner date. Coming along?

NORRIS [*gathering his things together*]: What about you, Dan?

HAYWOOD: I think I'll stay here a little while.

[*Ives and Norris exit. Haywood picks up one of Janning's books, begins leafing through it.*]

SCENE: PALACE OF JUSTICE—PRISON WAITING ROOM

[*Rolfe sits with Janning. It is the first time that they have really spoken at any length together. Janning has refused until now to discuss his case with counsel.*]

ROLFE: Are they treating you all right?

JANNING: Yes, they're treating me all right.

ROLFE: We still have some friends who have contact with the American authorities. I can tell them if they're not treating you all right.

JANNING: They're treating me all right.

ROLFE: Herr Janning. [*Pause.*] We are both in an embarrassing position. I know you didn't want me as your counsel. I know you didn't want anyone. I want to tell you something. Will you listen to me?

[*Janning looks at Rolfe.*]

I intend to represent your case with complete dignity. There will be no appeal to sentiment. There will be no placing yourself at the mercy of the court. The game will be played according to their own rules. We will see if they have the courage to sit in judgment on a man like you. [*Pause. Waits for a reply.*] Herr Janning. I have followed your career since I was a boy studying at the university. It was because I thought I might be able to achieve some of the things that you did that saw me through the war.

JANNING: How old are you?

ROLFE: Thirty-two.

JANNING: [*with wonder, remembering himself at that age*]: Thirty-two. Are you finished?

ROLFE: Yes.

[*Janning exits.*]

SCENE: PALACE OF JUSTICE—COURTROOM

[*Dr. Karl Wickert is on the stand. He is a distinguished looking man in his seventies. He walks with a cane. He had been Minister of Justice before Janning. His conflicts with Hitler are well known. He is living proof that a man could stand up to Hitler and still live.*]

COLONEL PARKER: Would you state your name to the Tribunal please?

DR. WICKERT: Karl Wickert.

COLONEL PARKER: Did you know the defendant, Ernst Janning?

DR. WICKERT: Yes. I know Ernst Janning.

COLONEL PARKER: Will you tell us in what capacity?

DR. WICKERT: We served in the Ministry of Justice together until 1935.

COLONEL PARKER: Did you know him before that?

DR. WICKERT: Yes. He was a law student of mine.

COLONEL PARKER: Did you know him well?

DR. WICKERT : Yes.

COLONEL PARKER: Was he a protégé of yours?

DR. WICKERT: Yes.

COLONEL PARKER: Dr. Wickert, will you tell us, from your own experience, the position of the judge in Germany prior to the advent of Adolf Hitler.

DR. WICKERT: The position of the judge was one of complete independence.

COLONEL PARKER: And did this system change after the Nazis came to power?

DR. WICKERT: Judges became subject to something outside of objective justice. They became subject to what was necessary for the protection of the country.

COLONEL PARKER: Would you explain this please?

DR. WICKERT: The first consideration of the judge became the punishment of acts against the State rather than the protection of the accused.

COLONEL PARKER: What other changes were there?

DR. WICKERT: The right to appeal was eliminated. The Supreme Court of the Reich was abolished. The concept of race was made a legal concept for the first time.

COLONEL PARKER: What was the result of this change?

DR. WICKERT: The result was to hand over the entire judicial system of the country into the hands of the dictator.

HAYWOOD [*interrupting*]: Dr. Wickert. I would like to ask you a question. Did the judges protest these laws abridging that independence?

DR. WICKERT: A few of them did. Those who did resigned or were forced to resign. Others ... Others adapted themselves to the new situation.

HAYWOOD: Do you think that the judiciary was aware of the consequences to come?

DR. WICKERT: At first, perhaps not. Then it became clear to anyone who had eyes and ears.

HAYWOOD: Thank you.

COLONEL PARKER: Dr. Wickert. Would you discuss for us the changes in criminal law that took place under the Third Reich?

DR. WICKERT: Special courts were established. These courts imposed the death penalty or heavy sentences whether the accused was guilty or not—only because they were Jews or Poles or politically unreliable. Also, novel National Socialist measures were introduced, among them sexual sterilization of those characterized as "asocial." All these things were done under the authority of Ernst Janning, as Minister of Justice.

COLONEL PARKER: Dr. Wickert, did it become necessary for judges to wear any distinctive mark on their robes in 1935?

DR. WICKERT: Yes. The so-called Führer's decree required judges to wear the insignia of the swastika on their robes.

COLONEL PARKER: Did you wear such an insignia?

DR. WICKERT: No. I would have been ashamed to wear it.

COLONEL PARKER: Did you resign in 1935?

DR. WICKERT: Yes.

COLONEL PARKER: Did Ernst Janning wear a swastika on his robe?

DR. WICKERT: Yes.

COLONEL PARKER: Thank you Dr. Wickert. That's all.

HAYWOOD: The defense counsel may cross-examine.

[*Rolfe rises and approaches Dr. Wickert cautiously. Dr. Wickert's reputation in Germany is an awesome one. Rolfe probes to find an ally in Wickert.*]

ROLFE: Dr. Wickert. You used the phrase, "What was necessary for the protection of the country." Would you explain for the Tribunal the conditions in Germany at the time National Socialism came to power?

DR. WICKERT: What conditions?

[*Rolfe pauses. He can see that Wickert will give him nothing.*]

ROLFE: Would you say there was wide-spread hunger?

DR. WICKERT: In 1933, yes.

ROLFE: Would you say there was internal disunity?

DR. WICKERT: Yes.

ROLFE: Would you say that National Socialism helped to cure some of these conditions?

DR. WICKERT: Yes, but at a terrible price!

ROLFE: Dr. Wickert, please confine yourself to answering the questions only. Therefore, was it not possible that a judge might wear a swastika and yet work for what he thought was best for his country?

DR. WICKERT: No, it was not possible.

ROLFE: Was there a Communist Party?

DR. WICKERT: Yes.

ROLFE: Was it the third largest party in Germany?

DR. WICKERT: Yes, it was.

ROLFE: Did they set fire to the Reichstag, one of Germany's most sacred buildings?

DR. WICKERT: That is one interpretation. My interpretation is that the Nazis set fire to it themselves to give the appearance of a national crisis so that they could take the system of justice away from the independent courts and put it in the hands of the dear Führer.

ROLFE: Dr. Wickert, you were not in the administration from the years 1935 to 1943 by your own admission. Is it not possible that your view of the administration might be distorted?

DR. WICKERT: No. It is not.

ROLFE: How can you testify to what was going on in the administration if you were not there?

DR. WICKERT: I had friends in the legal administration. There were books, journals.

ROLFE: From books and journals. I see. Dr. Wickert you refer to "novel national socialist measures introduced" among them sterilization. Are you aware sterilization was not invented by National Socialism, but has been advanced for years before as a weapon in dealing with the mentally incompetent and the criminal?

DR. WICKERT: Yes, I'm aware of that.

ROLFE: Are you aware that it has advocates among leading citizens in many other countries?

DR. WICKERT: I'm not an expert on sterilization laws!

ROLFE: Then permit me to read one to you. [*Picks up legal journal.*] This is a high court opinion, upholding a sterilization law in existence in another country. And I quote "We have seen more than once, that the public welfare may call upon the best citizens for their lives. It would be strange indeed if it could not call upon those who already sapped the strength of the State in order to prevent our being swamped by incompetence. It is better for all the world, if, instead of waiting to execute the general offspring for crime or to let them starve through their imbecility, society can—through sterilization—prevent those who are manifestly unfit for continuing their kind. Three generations of imbeciles are enough." End quote. [*Closes book with a snap.*] Do you recognize it now, Dr. Wickert?

DR. WICKERT: No, Sir. I do not.

ROLFE: Actually there is no particular reason you should since the opinion upholds the sterilization law in the State of Virginia of the United States, and was written and delivered by that great American jurist, Supreme Court Justice, Oliver Wendell Holmes. [*With satisfaction.*] Now Dr. Wickert, in view of what you have just learned, can you still say sexual sterilization was a novel National Socialist measure?

DR. WICKERT: Yes, I can say it! Because never before has it been used as weapon against political enemies!

ROLFE: Do you personally know of a case in which someone was sterilized for political reasons?

DR. WICKERT: I know such things were done!

ROLFE: Please answer the question. Do you know of a case?

DR. WICKERT: I do not know a specific name, or of a specific date.

ROLFE: That's not the question. I am asking you if you have any first hand, personal knowledge of such a case.

DR. WICKERT: No, Sir. I have no such personal knowledge.

ROLFE [trying once more to reach Dr. Wickert]: Dr. Wickert, are you aware of the charges in the indictment against Ernst Janning?

DR. WICKERT: Yes.

ROLFE [gently; trying to reach him]: Can you honestly say he is responsible for them?

DR. WICKERT: Yes, I can.

[There is a moment. Rolfe stares at Dr. Wickert, then proceeds in a direction he was hoping he would not have to. But as he does Rolfe reveals the deep emotion he has had about Dr. Wickert and people like him for years and been unable to express publicly.]

ROLFE: Dr. Wickert, do you consider yourself free of responsibility?

DR. WICKERT: Yes, I do.

ROLFE: Dr. Wickert, did you ever swear to the Civil Servant Loyalty Oath in 1934?

COLONEL PARKER: Your Honor, I object. The witness does not have to answer that question. He is not on trial.

ROLFE: All Germany is on trial, Your Honors. This Tribunal placed it on trial when it placed Ernst Janning on trial. If responsibility is to be found, the widest latitude is to be permitted.

HAYWOOD: Objection overruled.

ROLFE: Did you ever swear to the Civil Servant Loyalty Oath of 1934?

DR. WICKERT [*pausing*]: Everyone did.

ROLFE: We are not interested in what everyone did. We want to know what you did. I will read you the oath from the Reich Law Gazette, March 1933. "I swear that I shall be obedient to the leader of the German Reich and people, Adolf Hitler; that I shall be loyal to him; that I will observe the laws; and that I will conscientiously fulfill my duties, so help me God."

DR. WICKERT: Everyone swore to it. It was mandatory.

ROLFE: Yes. But you're a perceptive man, Dr. Wickert. You could see what was coming. You should see that National Socialism was leading Germany to disaster. "It was clear to anyone who had eyes and ears." Didn't you realize what it would have meant if you and men like you, had refused to swear to the oath? It would have meant that Hitler would never have come to absolute power. Why didn't you doctor?

[*Wickert is unable to reply.*]

Can you give us an explanation? Did it have something to do with your pension? Did your pension mean more to you than your country?

[*Dr. Wickert stares at him. It is a conclusion that he has dared not reach about himself.*]

COLONEL PARKER: Your Honor!

ROLFE: No further questions.

COLONEL PARKER: Your Honor, I object to the entire line of questioning and ask that it be stricken from the record!

ROLFE [*with irony*]: I thought the prosecuting council was dedicated to finding responsibility.

COLONEL PARKER: Your Honor I've made an objection.

ROLFE: Prosecution is not interested in finding responsibility?

COLONEL PARKER: There is responsibility for more here than swearing to a Loyalty Oath and you know it.

ROLFE: There is indeed. There's responsibility for heinous crimes. Crimes that have been charged against some of the most eminent men . . .

COLONEL PARKER: They are all eminent men. Every man who's been in the dock has been an eminent man.

ROLFE: Prosecution has stated it will prove responsibility by evidence . . .

COLONEL PARKER: Defense counsel may be speaking that way because he knows no one who was in the administration will step forward and speak the truth.

ROLFE: Your Honor!

COLONEL PARKER: There is one thing that even the German machine with its monumental efficiency has been unable to destroy . . .

HAYWOOD [*banging the gavel firmly*]: Order!

COLONEL PARKER: . . . all the victims. More victims than the world has ever known. They will walk into this court-room . . .

HAYWOOD: Tribunal will now admonish both counsel. It will tolerate nothing like this again. We are not here to listen to outbursts of this kind, but to serve justice. It will not be served by emotions of this kind.

COLONEL PARKER: Your Honor I made an objection.

HAYWOOD: Objection overruled! [*Bangs gavel.*] Court is adjourned until tomorrow morning.

[*Dr. Wickert still sits motionless in the witness box, stunned and humiliated.*]

You are excused.

[*Dr. Wickert still sits motionless.*]

HAYWOOD [*gently*]: You may go.

[*Dr. Wickert rises and walks out of the courtroom a different man than when he entered.*]

SCENE: JUDGE HAYWOOD'S QUARTERS

[*Mrs. Halbestadt, the housekeeper, native of Nuremberg, talks with Margarete Bertholt. Mrs. Halbestadt is in her early fifties. She has been a servant to General Bertholt and Mrs. Bertholt, who lived in the house. Mrs. Bertholt is in her forties. Tall, attractive in a rather athletic way. In spite of her capable and athletic look, there is something above all fragile about her. Her clothes are well tailored but they are obviously old. There is a box on the floor before her. It is a large box filled with items.*]

HAYWOOD: Mrs. Halbestadt, I wonder if I could have some— [*Surprised.*] Hello.

MRS. BERTHOLT: Hello.

MRS. HALBESTADT: Your Honor, this is Mrs. Bertholt. This is His Honor, Judge Haywood ... Mrs. Bertholt ... this was her house ... she came to get some of her belongings from the basement. I didn't know she was coming tonight or—

MRS. BERTHOLT: It's my responsibility, Mrs. Halbestadt. [*To Haywood.*] I have just been storing some things in the basement until I could get a room big enough to keep them. I hope you don't mind.

HAYWOOD: No. No not at all.

MRS. BERTHOLT: You can check what I have here if you like.

HAYWOOD: No. No. Of course not.

MRS. BERTHOLT: Thank you. I'll just take these out. Thank you, Mrs. Halbestadt.

HAYWOOD: Let me help you with that.

MRS. BERTHOLT: It's perfectly all right. I can manage. It's full of books and pictures and I don't know what. Things that mean nothing to anyone except to me.

HAYWOOD: Tell the driver to take her home.

MRS. HALBESTADT: Yes, Your Honor. I'll take it Mrs. Bertholt.

[*Mrs. Halbestadt exits with boxes.*]

MRS. BERTHOLT: Thank you. I hope you are comfortable here.

HAYWOOD [*awkwardly*]: Yes, I am. Very.

MRS. BERTHOLT: My favorite spot was always the garden. Remind Mrs. Halbestadt to take good care of it. You'll get a great deal of pleasure out of it in the summer. Good night.

HAYWOOD: Good night.

[*Mrs. Bertholt exits. Mrs. Halbestadt returns.*]

HAYWOOD: Mrs. Halbestadt, you worked for Mrs. Bertholt. Didn't you?

MRS. HALBESTADT [*warily*]: Yes, Your Honor.

HAYWOOD: How long did she live here?

MRS. HALBESTADT: Mrs. Bertholt and her family have lived here for generations, Your Honor.

HAYWOOD: Thanks.

MRS. HALBESTADT: Your Honor, you came in here for something.

HAYWOOD: Yes I was going to make myself a sandwich.

MRS. HALBESTADT: I'll make it for you, Your Honor. I'll make anything you want.

HAYWOOD: No. It's nothing. I always did it for myself back home.

MRS. HALBESTADT: What would you like? We have some ham and some tongue and some liver sausage.

HAYWOOD: I'll try that liver sausage.

[*Mrs. Halbestadt starts preparing the sandwich.*]

That's very kind of you. What was it like to live under National Socialism?

MRS. HALBESTADT: What was it like?

HAYWOOD: What was it like day to day? You're just like people back home. You're good people, I know that. What was it like for you to live under Hitler?

MRS. HALBESTADT: We were not political. I am not political.

HAYWOOD: I know, but you must have been aware of some of the events that were going on. A lot of things were going on. There were parades going on. Hitler and Goebbels used to come here every year. What was it like?

MRS. HALBESTADT: We never attended meetings. Never.

HAYWOOD: I'm not putting you on trial, Mrs. Halbestadt. I just would like to know.

[*Mrs. Halbestadt finishes making the sandwich and places it before him.*]

Thank you.

MRS. HALBESTADT: You're welcome, Your Honor.

HAYWOOD: For instance, there's a place just 80 miles from here called Dachau.

MRS. HALBESTADT: We knew nothing about it. Nothing about it. How can you ask if we knew anything about it? [*She is on the point of tears.*]

HAYWOOD: I'm sorry.

[*He starts to eat the sandwich.*]

MRS. HALBESTADT: Is the sandwich all right, Your Honor?

HAYWOOD: Yes, it's fine thank you.

MRS. HALBESTADT: Your Honor, we are just little people. I lost a son in the war. I lost a daughter in the bombing. We went hungry during the war. It was terrible for us.

HAYWOOD: I'm sure it was.

MRS. HALBESTADT: Hitler did some good things. I won't say he didn't do some good things. He gave more people work. I won't say he didn't do some good things. But the bad things—the things they say he did to the Jews and the rest. We didn't know about such things. Very few Germans knew. [*Pause.*] And if we did know, what could we do?

HAYWOOD: But Mrs. Halbestadt. You said you didn't know. [*Pause.*] Mrs. Bertholt. What was Mrs. Bertholt's reaction to all of this?

MRS. HALBESTADT: Mrs. Bertholt is a very fine woman, Your Honor.

HAYWOOD: What about her husband?

MRS. HALBESTADT: He was in the Army.

HAYWOOD: Oh? What happened to him?

MRS. HALBESTADT: He was a defendant in the Malmedy Case, Your Honor.

HAYWOOD: General Bertholt? Karl Bertholt.

MRS. HALBESTADT: He was executed, Your Honor.

HAYWOOD: Yes, I know that.

SCENE: THE PALACE OF JUSTICE—COURTROOM

COLONEL PARKER: "The seamstress Anni Meunch, daughter of Wilhelm Meunch is to be sterilized. It is therefore requested—"

ROLFE: Your Honor, Defense objects to introduction of these documents. According to the ruling of the first Tribunal, such documents are not admissible unless supported by independent evidence of their authenticity.

HAYWOOD: Objection sustained.

COLONEL PARKER: Your Honor, may I ask the Defense a question? Would evidence on sterilization be acceptable if there were a witness.

[*Pause.*]

ROLFE [*apprehensively*]: Yes. It would.

[*Colonel Parker abruptly throws documentation in front of Rolfe. Rolfe continues reading documentation through Peterson's testimony.*]

COLONEL PARKER: Prosecution calls the witness, Rudolph Peterson.

[*Rudolf Peterson is in his thirties. Suit worn but carefully pressed. Hair carefully combed. He seems to be holding himself together with difficulty.*]

CAPT. BYERS: Will you raise your right hand and repeat after me the following oath: I swear by God, the Almighty and omniscient that I will speak the pure truth and will withhold and add nothing.

PETERSON: I swear by God, the Almighty and omniscient, that I will speak the pure truth and will withhold and add nothing.

COLONEL PARKER: Will you please tell the court your full name and place of residence.

PETERSON: Rudolph Peterson. Frankfurt am Main.

COLONEL PARKER: And what is your occupation?

PETERSON: I, I'm a baker's helper.

COLONEL PARKER: Are your parents living?

PETERSON: No they are not.

COLONEL PARKER: What were the causes of their deaths?

[*Peterson is confused.*]

Were they natural causes?

PETERSON: Yes natural causes.

COLONEL PARKER: Mr. Peterson. To what political party did your parents belong in 1933?

PETERSON: Um, the Communist Party.

COLONEL PARKER: And how old were you at the time?

PETERSON: About seventeen.

COLONEL PARKER: Now, Mr. Peterson, do you remember anything unusual that happened in 1933, before the Nazis came to power?

PETERSON: Um, yes, yes, Sir. Some S.A. men broke into our house. They smashed all the doors and the windows and um, called us all traitors and beat up my father. Me and my brothers drove the S.A. men out of the house and turned them over to the police.

COLONEL PARKER: Did the police do anything about the matter?

PETERSON: No.

COLONEL PARKER: Why not?

PETERSON: They had elections—at that time. The National Socialists had come to power.

COLONEL PARKER: And now would you tell the Tribunal what happened after 1933? When the Nazis had come to power?

PETERSON: I got a job on a farm, but for the work it was

necessary to drive a truck. I went to the town hall to apply for a license.

COLONEL PARKER: And what happened?

PETERSON: They took me to an official. He was one of the men who broke into our house. He told me that an examination would be necessary.

COLONEL PARKER: Where was the examination to take place?

PETERSON: In the district court of Stuttgart.

COLONEL PARKER: And who was the presiding judge in this court?

PETERSON: Justice Frederick Hoffstetter.

COLONEL PARKER: What happened in the courtroom?

PETERSON: They asked me when Adolf Hitler and Dr. Goebbels were born.

COLONEL PARKER: And what did you reply?

PETERSON: I, I told them that I didn't know and I didn't care either.

[*There is a ripple of laughter in the courtroom. It seems to buoy up Peterson's confidence a little. He smiles at the spectators in the courtroom who have laughed.*]

COLONEL PARKER: Mr. Peterson, do you recognize this piece of paper?

PETERSON: Yes, Sir, yes I do.

COLONEL PARKER: Would you read it to the Tribunal?

PETERSON [*reads slowly, stuttering*]: "District Court of Stuttgart. You are requested to present yourself within two weeks at one of the hospitals mentioned before to be sterilized. If you do not betake yourself voluntarily, you will be taken by force."

COLONEL PARKER: Now, Mr. Peterson would you read what is written below Justice Hoffstetter's signature.

PETERSON: Yes. "By the authority of Ernst Janning, Ministry of Justice."

COLONEL PARKER: Mr. Peterson, what did you do after you received this letter?

PETERSON: I, I ran away. But the police came and got me and took me to a hospital.

COLONEL PARKER: And what happened at the hospital?

PETERSON: They kept me there by force. A nurse came in who was supposed to prepare me for the operation and she told me that the whole thing was terrible. Then the doctor came in, who was supposed to operate on me, and told me that, that the whole thing was a shame—a disgrace.

COLONEL PARKER: And were you in fact sterilized?

PETERSON: Yes, Sir.

COLONEL PARKER: That's all.

HAYWOOD: Defense counsel will cross-examine.

ROLFE: Mr. Peterson. You worked as a baker's helper.

PETERSON: Yes.

ROLFE: And what other occupations have you held?

PETERSON: I have worked for my father.

ROLFE: What did your father do?

PETERSON: He was a railroad worker.

ROLFE: What did he do?

PETERSON: He carried signal cards on the railroads.

ROLFE: Mr. Peterson. You spoke about your brothers. How many brothers do you have?

PETERSON: Five.

ROLFE: How many sisters?

PETERSON: Four.

ROLFE: Four. Then you are a family of ten.

PETERSON: Yes. Ten.

ROLFE: What occupation do your brothers have?

PETERSON: They are all laborers.

ROLFE: Laborers. I see. How long did you attend school, Mr. Peterson?

PETERSON: Six years.

ROLFE: Six years? Why not longer?

PETERSON: I didn't want to attend longer. I wanted to go to work.

ROLFE: Would you consider yourself a very bright fellow at school?

PETERSON: I don't remember what happened at school.

ROLFE: Your Honor, I offer as evidence the petition that came from the court in Stuttgart. I would like to read to you the efficiency report made at the school about Mr. Peterson. He failed to be promoted and was placed in a class of backward children.

COLONEL PARKER: Objection Your Honor. The witness's school record has nothing to do with his sterilization.

ROLFE: It was the task of the Health Court to order sterilization of the mentally incompetent.

HAYWOOD: Objection overruled.

ROLFE: Did your parents die of natural causes?

PETERSON: Yes.

ROLFE: Would you describe the illness your mother died of.

PETERSON: She died of heart disease.

ROLFE: During the last stages of her illness, did your mother show any mental peculiarities?

PETERSON: No.

ROLFE: In a decision that came from the court in Stuttgart, it is stated that your mother suffered from hereditary feeble-mindedness.

PETERSON: That's a lie!

ROLFE: Could you give us some clarification as to how the Hereditary Health Court at Stuttgart arrived at that decision?

PETERSON: It was just something they said to get me on the operating table.

ROLFE: It was just something they said. Mr. Peterson. You said, the court in Stuttgart asked you two questions. The birth date of Hitler and Dr. Goebbels?

PETERSON: Yes.

ROLFE: What else did they ask you?

PETERSON: Nothing else.

ROLFE: Are you sure?

PETERSON: Yes I am sure.

ROLFE: Mr. Peterson, there was a simple test that the court used to ask in all cases of possible mental incompetence. Since you say they did not ask you then, perhaps you can answer it now. Form a sentence out of the words: hare, hunter and field.

COLONEL PARKER: Objection, Your Honors.

HAYWOOD: Mr. Peterson, was the court at Stuttgart constituted like this? Was there an audience?

PETERSON: Yes, Sir. There was an audience.

HAYWOOD: Objection overruled.

ROLFE: Hare, hunter and field, Mr. Peterson. Take your time.

PETERSON: Hare, hunter and field . . . hare hunter field. [*Turns toward judges.*] They all made up their minds before I entered the courtroom they all made up their minds! They took me to that hospital and kept me there just like a criminal and I couldn't say anything! I just had to lay there. [*Stands up, shouting, turns to Rolfe.*] My mother was a hard working, very good woman all her life! It's not fair to say things about her! [*Turns to Haywood.*] I have a picture. [*Walks out of the witness box towards the judges' bench, pleading, crying.*] I would like to show it to you. I would like you to look at it. I would like you to judge whether my mother was feebleminded or not. I want you to tell me if she was feebleminded. My mother! Was she feebleminded? Was she? [*Crying.*]

ROLFE: It is my duty to point out to the Tribunal that the witness is not in control of his mental processes.

PETERSON: I am not! I know I am not! Since that day I am half of what I've ever been but I wasn't this way before.

ROLFE: The Tribunal does not know the way you were before. It can never know. It has only your word.

[*Rolfe walks slowly from the stand back to the dock. There is no pride in his walk.*]

SCENE: BAR IN THE GRAND HOTEL

[*Ives and Haywood are sitting. Ives is eating a plate of strudel. Sounds of music from an orchestra in the hotel drift in. It is an echo of the kind of music that was played during the Third Reich: waltzes, themes from threadbare operettas.*]

IVES: They have the greatest strudel I've ever tasted here.

HAYWOOD: It's good. But I'm getting a little bit tired of it. And little bit with the music, too. Don't they ever change their repertoire? I must have heard this tune a thousand times.

[*Mrs. Bertholt passes.*]

IVES: Just a minute. Mrs. Bertholt! Won't you come over? [*To Haywood.*] This is Mrs. Bertholt. Judge Haywood.

MRS. BERTHOLT: We've met. Hello.

HAYWOOD: Hello again.

IVES: Won't you join us for a drink?

MRS. BERTHOLT: Oh, thank you.

HAYWOOD: Please do. What would you like?

MRS. BERTHOLT: What are you having?

HAYWOOD: Well I've had my fill of beer. So I—

MRS. BERTHOLT: Why don't you try a local wine? Sonnenberg or Schwalbenwinkel?

HAYWOOD: Schwal . . .

MRS. BERTHOLT [smiles]: Schwalbenwinkel.

HAYWOOD [to Waiter]: I'll have some of that.

MRS BERTHOLT: I'll have the same. Thank you.

[Waiter exits.]

HAYWOOD: I hope you got home all right that night.

MRS. BERTHOLT: Yes, I did. Thank you. I don't know how I would have managed without the car.

HAYWOOD: You speak English very well.

MRS. BERTHOLT: My husband and I spent some years in America.

HAYWOOD: Really?

MRS. BERTHOLT: I hope you've been able to see some of Nuremberg.

HAYWOOD: Mainly the road from my house—from your house to the Palace of Justice. And the parts that deal with the case, of course. [Awkwardly.] The historical aspects.

MRS. BERTHOLT [*smiling*]: The Nazi aspects. You should see some of the other parts. It's been here a long time. Long before Hitler.

HAYWOOD: I was in the old section . . . once. We've been so busy. What would you suggest?

MRS. BERTHOLT: There's the Market Square. And there are many beautiful things in the old part of Nuremberg. There are even museums we are trying to rebuild. [*Pause.*] If you like classical music there is a piano concert next week at the old Opera House. Arthur Reiss. He was a refugee from Hitler in the early days. The committee persuaded him to come back. It ought to be quite an evening. Would you like to come?

HAYWOOD: Yes I would.

MRS. BERTHOLT: I'll tell them to leave a ticket at the box office for you. I'm on the committee.

HAYWOOD: Thank you very much, Mrs. Bertholt.

MRS. BERTHOLT: It's nothing. You see, I have a mission with Americans.

HAYWOOD: What's that?

MRS. BERTHOLT: To convince you that we're not all monsters.

[*Colonel Parker enters. It is obvious he has been drinking.*]

HAYWOOD: Good evening, Colonel.

COLONEL PARKER: Good evening, Mrs. Bertholt.

MRS. BERTHOLT [*quietly, color draining from her face*]: I hope you'll excuse me.

HAYWOOD: But you've just come, Mrs. Bertholt.

MRS. BERTHOLT: I must go. Please excuse me. Goodnight.

HAYWOOD: Goodnight.

[*She leaves.*]

COLONEL PARKER [*sitting down*]: Mrs. Bertholt doesn't harbor a burning passion for me. I prosecuted her husband.

IVES: There are many people who think that a death sentence wouldn't be passed against General Bertholt today.

COLONEL PARKER: I'm sure there are. I'm sure there are people who think that all the prisoners in Nuremberg should be free today. [*Stops.*] I've had one or two too many, as might be painfully obvious to you . . . The spectacle this afternoon with Mr. Peterson put me off my feed. Sorry.

IVES: The trouble with you, Colonel, is that you'd like to indict the whole country. That might be emotionally satisfying for you, but it's not exactly practical. And hardly fair.

[*Pause.*]

COLONEL PARKER: Hare, hunter, field. Let's be fair. The hare was shot by the hunter in the field. It's really quite simple.

IVES: We really shouldn't be discussing this, Colonel.

COLONEL PARKER: There are no Nazis in Germany. Didn't you know that, Judge? The Eskimos invaded Germany and took over. That's how all those terrible things happened. It wasn't the fault of the Germans. It was those damn Eskimos! [*He exits.*]

IVES: You know, that's one problem with the prosecution. It's filled with radicals like Parker.

HAYWOOD: Is that what Colonel Parker is, a radical?

IVES: He was a personal protégé of F.D.R.

HAYWOOD: That makes him a radical?

IVES: As a matter of fact I've been wondering how you stand, Dan.

HAYWOOD: I'll clarify that for you, Curtiss. I'm a rock-ribbed, southern Republican who thinks Roosevelt was a great man.

IVES: Oh. One of those.

[*There is a commotion in the lobby. Norris enters.*]

NORRIS: Did you hear what's going on?

IVES: What?

NORRIS: The Russians have entered Czechoslovakia. President Masaryk's committed suicide.

HAYWOOD: Good God.

NORRIS: The country's under martial law. We're sending some units up to the border. [*He exits.*]

IVES: Well this is it. The end of the grand alliance. I knew it was coming anyway.

NORRIS: Curtiss, I wonder whether we should send our wives home.

HAYWOOD: It's not that bad yet, Ken, is it?

NORRIS: The Czech border is only sixty miles away.

IVES: Supposing they decide to come over the border.

HAYWOOD: They're not saying they're going to do that, are they?

IVES: What difference does it make what they say? Nobody thought they'd take over Czechoslovakia. I always thought this was the real danger, anyway.

HAYWOOD: What the hell does that mean?

IVES: We should have kept out of the whole thing and let them destroy each other.

HAYWOOD: That is an interesting viewpoint, Curtiss.

IVES: Where has it gotten us? We're in for a life and death struggle. And who is the key to who wins that struggle? Germany. Any high school student in geography can tell you that.

[*Waiter approaches.*]

WAITER: More strudel, gentlemen?

END OF ACT I

ACT TWO

SCENE: THE PALACE OF JUSTICE—PRISON COURTYARD

[*Hoffstetter and Lammpe sit on benches. Janning sits on a bench apart from them. Hahn enters. He has a copy of* Stars and Stripes, *the U.S. Army publication, in his hand.*]

HAHN: Did you hear the news?

JANNING: What news?

HOFFSTETTER: Truman's speech.

JANNING: I'm not very interested in what Mr. Truman has to say.

HAHN: You'll be interested in this: "President Truman stated that since the Czechoslovakian crisis, he has become deeply concerned with the survival of the western nations in face of the threat from the East." [*Pause. Lowers paper.*] Threat from the East . . . Survival of the western nations. Just as Hitler said. The clash for survival between East and West. He knew. He knew. [*Pause.*] Ernst, you were the head of the judiciary. You have followers not only in Germany but all over the world. If you get up and speak, the world will listen. [*Pause.*] You must get up and speak, do you understand me?

JANNING: We have fallen on good times, haven't we, Herr Hahn? In the old times it would have made your day if I had deigned to say "good morning" to you. Now that we are in this place together, you feel obliged to order me what to do with my life.

HAHN: We must stand together now. The most crucial part of the case is coming up now. They cannot call us criminals and at the same time ask us to help them. You must stand with us. It's not good for Germans to turn on one another. It will not be good for them to see that now. We must stand together now. We have common ground now.

JANNING: What common ground do we have? What do I have in common with you and the rest of the Party hacks like you? Listen to me, Herr Hahn. There were terrible things that happened to me in my life, but the worst thing that has ever happened is that I find myself in the company of men like you.

HAHN: You have something in common. You were part of the same regime. You stood by that regime the same as the rest of us. [*Pause.*] There is something else you have in common. You are a German.

SCENE: MRS. BERTHOLT'S ROOM

[*It is fairly bare, but whatever furniture there is is very tasteful. There has obviously been very much done with very little. Mrs. Bertholt enters followed by Haywood. They have come from the Opera House. Haywood looks at the small room, obviously struck by the fact that Mrs. Bertholt is living in this small room while he is living in her old house with such enormous space.*]

MRS. BERTHOLT: Let me have your coat. It's a little warmer here than in the Opera House. I'll put on the coffee. It will be ready in a minute.

[*Haywood gives her his coat. Mrs. Bertholt hangs it up.*]

It's quite empty at the moment but I've really just started. I'm going to have the dining room in the alcove. I'll get a small piano and put it over there. I have a beautiful painting by Feininger. Do you know Feininger's work?

HAYWOOD: No. No. I don't.

MRS. BERTHOLT: It's lovely. Germans are always talking about their possessions, aren't they? What's life like for you back home?

HAYWOOD: What's it like?

MRS. BERTHOLT: Please. Sit down. What kind of position do you hold? Is it very important?

HAYWOOD: No. No. Not very important at all. I'm a district court judge that's all. And for the last year or so, I haven't even been that.

MRS. BERTHOLT: You are retired?

HAYWOOD: Forcibly. By the electorate.

MRS. BERTHOLT: You elect judges in the United States?

HAYWOOD: Yes. We do. In some districts.

MRS. BERTHOLT: I didn't know that.

HAYWOOD: It's either one of the virtues of our judiciary system or one of the defects. I thought it was one of the virtues until I was defeated last year.

MRS. BERTHOLT: I'm sure it was the electorate's fault, not yours.

HAYWOOD: There seems to be a difference of opinion about that. I don't know. I was in a long time. I guess they just got tired of me, that's all. A new fellow came along. What about you, Mrs. Bertholt? You said you were in the United States. Where?

MRS. BERTHOLT: My husband and I took a ride by automobile all over the United States. We were really very impressed. It was a very happy time for us. The coffee must be ready. I'll get it.

[*Goes to kitchen. Haywood follows.*]

HAYWOOD: What impressed you most?

MRS. BERTHOLT: The people. They are so outgoing, so really uncomplicated. People in Germany think it's an act. But that's because they don't know Americans. They really are like that. Do you take milk and sugar?

HAYWOOD: Black. Life isn't easy for you now, is it?

MRS. BERTHOLT: I'm not used to life being easy. I'm a daughter of the military. You know what that means, don't you?

[*They go into next room.*]

HAYWOOD: No, I'm afraid I don't.

MRS. BERTHOLT: It means that I was taught discipline in a very special way. For instance: when I was a child we used to go for long hikes in the country, but I would never be allowed to run to the lemonade stands with the others. "Control your thirst," I was told. Control hunger. Control emotions. It has served me well.

HAYWOOD: Was your husband like that? Was he part of that heritage too?

MRS. BERTHOLT: He was a soldier. Brought up to do one thing. To fight in the battle and fight well.

[*There is a moment. Mrs. Bertholt waits until Haywood tries his coffee. Haywood tastes it.*]

Do you have a family, Judge Haywood?

HAYWOOD: Yes, I do. I have a daughter. She has four children.

MRS. BERTHOLT: Where's Mrs. Haywood?

HAYWOOD: She died a few years ago. How about you. Do you have children?

MRS. BERTHOLT: No. I don't. [*Pause.*] I'm curious. What are your feelings about Ernst Janning?

HAYWOOD: I'm sorry, Mrs. Bertholt. I can't discuss the case at all outside the court.

MRS. BERTHOLT: Yes. Of course. It was just that I knew Ernst Janning a little. We used to attend the same concerts. I remember there was a reception given for Wagner's daughter-in-law. Hitler was there. Janning was there with his wife also. She was very beautiful, very small, very delicate. She is dead now. Hitler seemed quite taken with her. He made advances toward her at the reception.

HAYWOOD: Hitler?

MRS. BERTHOLT [*nods*]: He would do things like that in a burst of emotion. I will never forget the way Janning cut him down. I don't think anybody ever did it quite that way to him. He said, "Chancellor, I do not object so much that you are ill-mannered. I do not object to that so much. I do object that you are such a bourgeois."

HAYWOOD: What happened?

MRS. BERTHOLT: Hitler's face whitened. He just stared at Janning and then walked out. Would you like some more coffee?

HAYWOOD: No, I'm fine.

MRS. BERTHOLT: Men like Janning and my husband and I, we hated Hitler. I want you to know that. And he hated us. He hated my husband because he was a real war hero and the little corporal couldn't tolerate that. Because he married into the nobility which was my family. Hitler was in awe of the nobility, but he hated it. That's why it was so outrageous what happened. You know what happened to my husband?

HAYWOOD: Yes.

MRS. BERTHOLT: What did he know about the crimes they cited him for? He was placed on trial with the Nazi political leaders and he was made to seem one of them. He became part of the revenge the victors always take on the vanquished. It was political murder. You know that, don't you?

HAYWOOD: I don't know what I believe, Mrs. Bertholt.

MRS. BERTHOLT: You don't know what to believe. No. All of us don't know what to believe. We're each told lies about each other. If you go to either side, you'll hear about atrocities of the other. I wish the day will come when there will be no more lies. I have the case on my husband here. Would you like to read it?

HAYWOOD: No. No, Mrs. Bertholt.

MRS. BERTHOLT: You don't want to read it?

HAYWOOD: Mrs. Bertholt, I shouldn't be listening to this. I shouldn't even be here. I should get everything I need out of the courtroom. [*With emotion.*] But I don't. So I look for the answers in the streets. In the Opera House. In the cafés. On the streetcars. They all seem like human beings like any human beings. But inhuman things happened here. What the hell happened in this country?!

SCENE: PALACE OF JUSTICE—COURTROOM

[*Dr. Geuter is on the stand. He is a soft-spoken man in his fifties.*]

COLONEL PARKER: Do you recognize this headline?

DR. GEUTER: Yes Sir.

COLONEL PARKER: Will you read it to the Tribunal?

DR. GEUTER [*reads*]: "Death to the Race Defiler"

COLONEL PARKER: In what newspaper did this appear?

DR. GEUTER: In Julius Streicher's *Der Stuermer* in connection with the Feldenstein case.

COLONEL PARKER: And what was the Feldenstein case?

DR. GEUTER: The case of a man here in Nuremberg charged with "racial pollution."

COLONEL PARKER: Will you explain to the Tribunal what is meant by "racial pollution?"

DR. GEUTER: It is referred to in the Nuremberg laws. It says that any non-Aryan having sexual relations with an Aryan may be punished by death.

COLONEL PARKER: Dr. Geuter. When did you first become acquainted with the Feldenstein case?

DR. GEUTER: The police contacted me in September 1935. They said that Lehman Feldenstein was being held. And that he had asked me to represent him as counsel.

COLONEL PARKER: Had you known him before?

DR. GEUTER: Yes. Very well.

COLONEL PARKER: What position did he hold in the community?

DR. GEUTER: He was a well-known merchant and one of the heads of the Jewish congregation of Nuremberg.

COLONEL PARKER: And what was the nature of the charge against him?

DR. GEUTER: He was accused of having intimate relations with a sixteen-year-old girl, Maria Wallner.

COLONEL PARKER: Did you go to see Mr. Feldenstein?

DR. GEUTER: Yes.

COLONEL PARKER: What did Mr. Feldenstein say to you about the case?

DR. GEUTER: He said it was false. He said that he had known a girl and her family a long time and had visited her since they died. But there had never been anything of that kind between them.

COLONEL PARKER: Will you tell the Tribunal what happened then?

DR. GEUTER: Mr. Feldenstein was indicted before the special court at Nuremberg.

COLONEL PARKER: Where was the special court?

DR. GEUTER: It was here. In this building. In this very courtroom.

COLONEL PARKER: What were the circumstances surrounding the trial?

DR. GEUTER: It was used as a showcase for National Socialism. It was the time of the September celebrations. The Nuremberg rallies. The courtroom was packed. There were people standing back there. Julius Streicher was sitting in one of those front seats with the members of the S.A. all around him.

COLONEL PARKER: What were your expectations for the trial in this climate?

DR. GEUTER: I expected the worst when I saw Emil Hahn was public prosecutor. He was a fanatic. His trials were always marked by his brutality. But I still had some hope for the outcome because sitting on the judge's bench was Ernst Janning.

COLONEL PARKER: Thank you, Dr. Geuter. That's all.

HAYWOOD: Defense counsel may cross-examine.

ROLFE: Thank you. No questions.

HAYWOOD: The witness is excused.

[*Dr. Geuter rises and exits through the door.*]

COLONEL PARKER: The prosecution calls to the stand Miss Maria Wallner.

[*Maria Wallner, in her thirties, enters. There is evidence that she was once an attractive woman, but what is left is the shadow of what she must have been. We feel that some traumatic event has marked her deeply. She looks over at the men in the dock with fascination that she is seeing them here in this place and that they are defendants.]*

COLONEL PARKER: Will you please state your name to the Tribunal?

MARIA: Maria Wallner.

COLONEL PARKER: Miss Wallner, did you know Lehman Feldenstein?

MARIA: Yes.

COLONEL PARKER: When did you first know him?

MARIA: Since I was five or six years old. I'm not sure exactly.

COLONEL PARKER: How old was he at this time?

MARIA: He must have been in his fifties.

COLONEL PARKER: How old was he at the time of his arrest?

MARIA: He was sixty-five.

COLONEL PARKER: What was the nature of your relationship?

MARIA: We were friends.

COLONEL PARKER: Did you continue to see him after your parents died?

MARIA: Yes.

COLONEL PARKER: Why?

MARIA: We were friends. He owned the building I lived in. His business took him there quite often.

COLONEL PARKER: What did you say to the police, when they questioned you about having intimate relations with him?

MARIA: I told them it was a lie.

COLONEL PARKER: Could you tell me who the public prosecutor was?

[*Maria looks toward Hahn in the dock. In her face is fear. There is also the fascination for this monster being in the dock. This man who spoke so solemnly and so piously about his own brand of righteousness.*]

MARIA: It was Emil Hahn.

COLONEL PARKER: Did the public prosecutor question you?

MARIA: Yes.

COLONEL PARKER: What did he say to you?

MARIA: He took me into a separate room where we were alone. He told me that there was no use repeating my story because no one would believe me. There had been race defilement and the only pardon for this was in killing the violator. He said if I protected Mr. Feldenstein I would be held under arrest for perjury.

COLONEL PARKER: What did you reply to him?

MARIA: I told him what I had said again and again. I told him I could not say anything else. I could not lie about someone who had been so kind to me.

COLONEL PARKER: Were you held under arrest?

MARIA: Yes.

COLONEL PARKER: What was the manner in which Emil Hahn conducted the prosecution?

MARIA: He mocked everything Mr. Feldenstein tried to say in his defense. He used every opportunity to hold him up to ridicule.

COLONEL PARKER: What was the reaction of the audience?

MARIA: They laughed again and again.

COLONEL PARKER: How long did the trial last?

MARIA: Two days.

COLONEL PARKER: Was the verdict passed at the end of the second day?

MARIA: Yes.

COLONEL PARKER: What was the verdict?

MARIA: Guilty.

COLONEL PARKER: What was the sentence?

MARIA: Mr. Feldenstein was sentenced to be executed. I was sentenced to be imprisoned for two years for perjury.

COLONEL PARKER: Who was the presiding judge?

MARIA: Ernst Janning.

COLONEL PARKER: Were the sentences carried out?

MARIA: Yes.

COLONEL PARKER: Miss Wallner, it was not easy for you to come here and testify today, was it?

MARIA: People do not think Germans should testify against other Germans.

COLONEL PARKER: But you have come? Why?

MARIA: I came for Lehman Feldenstein.

COLONEL PARKER: That's all.

HAYWOOD: Cross-examination?

ROLFE: Your Honor, I would like to request that the witness be kept available. We will present further evidence on the Feldenstein case when it comes to the time for the defense to present its case.

HAYWOOD: The witness will remain available. Prosecution will continue.

COLONEL PARKER: Thank you, Your Honor. The prosecution will conclude its case with the evidence which I am about to offer. [*Looks at men in dock.*] The defendants on trial here today did not personally administer the concentration camps. They never had to beat victims or pull the levers in the gas chambers. But as the documents and testimony we have introduced have shown, these defendants issued the orders and rendered judgments which sent millions of victims to their terrible destinations. Your Honors, there are no words to fully describe what happened. But we have a mute but eloquent witness . . . the camera's eye. I now respectfully request the Tribunal to view what the camera saw.

[*The MP wheels in a projector. The MP switches on the projector.*

The screen is lowered. Documentary film footage from the Signal Corps is shown.]

COLONEL PARKER: This map shows the number and location of concentration camps under the Third Reich. Buchenwald concentration camp was founded in 1933. The inmates at the camp numbered about 80,000. There was a motto at Buchenwald: "Break the body. Break the spirit. Break the heart." The ovens at Buchenwald, the evidence of last-minute efforts to dispose of bodies. An exhibit of the by-products of Buchenwald was displayed for the local townspeople. A lampshade made of human skin. Human skin being used for paintings; many of an obscene nature. The heads of two Polish laborers shrunken to one fifth their normal size. A human pelvis used as an ashtray is displayed. Children who have been tattooed to mark them for eventual extermination. Hundreds of inmates were used as human guinea pigs for atrocious medical experiments. A witness of one of the executions of Dachau gave the following description: "Inmates were made to leave their clothing on a rack. The inmates were made to believe they were going to take showers. The doors were locked. Gasses called *Zyclon B* were released through the specially constructed apertures. This is what was found when British troops liberated the Belsen concentration camp. For sanitary reasons, the bulldozer is forced to bury the bodies as quickly as possible. Who were the bodies? 200,000 mentally and physically disabled. 220,000 Gypsies. 3 million Soviet P.O.W.'s. Two thirds of the Jews of Europe exterminated; more than six million according to reports compiled from the Nazis' own figures. But the real figures no one knows.

SCENE: LOBBY, GRAND HOTEL

[*Haywood and Mrs. Bertholt sit at a table. Mrs. Bertholt has circulars before her. Haywood is still stunned by the films he has seen in the courtroom.*]

MRS. BERTHOLT: I brought down these guides and maps for you. We can decide what you should see next. You must see the Albrecht Dürer house. And the museum. When do you think you could make it?

HAYWOOD: Oh. Any weekend.

MRS. BERTHOLT: What would you like?

HAYWOOD: I don't think I'll have anything.

MRS. BERTHOLT: Just a glass of Moselle, please. [*To Haywood.*] What's the matter?

HAYWOOD: I'm just not very thirsty, that's all. [*Pause.*] You know. These last few days have meant a lot to me.

MRS. BERTHOLT: How?

HAYWOOD: Well, I don't think you realize what a provincial man I am. I've been abroad exactly once before. When I was a doughboy in World War I. I used to pass places like this and wonder what they were really like.

MRS. BERTHOLT: They've meant a lot to me too.

HAYWOOD: How?

MRS. BERTHOLT: They've given back to me the feelings of the Americans I had. The feeling I had when I went to your country.

[*Waiter brings glass of wine for Mrs. Bertholt. She sips from it.*]

I saw someone who worked in the court today. He told me they showed those pictures in the courtroom. Colonel Parker and his pictures. He drags them out on any pretext, doesn't he? Colonel Parker's private chamber of horrors. Well. Is that the way you think we are? Do you think we were aware of those things? Do you think we wanted to murder women and children? Do you believe that? Do you?

HAYWOOD: Margarete, I don't know what to believe.

MRS. BERTHOLT: Dan. My God. We're sitting here drinking. You don't know much about me but we have experienced a few things together. How can you think that we knew?

HAYWOOD: As far as I can find out, no one in this country knew. Your husband was one of the heads of the Army—

MRS. BERTHOLT: He didn't know! I tell you he didn't know! It was Himmler. It was Goebbels. The S.S. knew what was happening. We didn't know. Listen. Listen to me. There are things that happened on both sides. My husband was a military man all his life. He was entitled to a soldier's death. He asked for that. I tried to get that for him. Just that. That he should die with some honor. I went from official to official. I asked for that. I begged for that. Just that he be permitted the dignity of a firing squad. You know what happened. He was hanged with the others. After that I knew what it meant to hate. I never left the house. I never left my room. I drank. I hated with every fiber of my being. I hated every American I had ever known. Dan. One can't live with hate! I've learned that. Dan. Dan. We have to forget! We have to forget if we are to go on living!

SCENE: PALACE OF JUSTICE—COURTROOM

[*Rolfe rises. It is obvious he has been shaken by the films that have been shown. It is also obvious he is trying to keep his emotions in check.*]

ROLFE: Your Honor. [*Pause.*] Yesterday the Tribunal witnessed some films. They were shocking films. Devastating films. [*Quietly.*] As a German I am ashamed that such things could take place in my country. There can never be a justification for them. Not in generations. Not in centuries. [*Pause; the emotions coming through.*] But I do think it was terribly unfair to show these films—in this case, at this time, against these defendants! [*Turns to look at Colonel Parker.*] And I cannot protest too strongly against such tactics! [*To Judges.*] What is the prosecution trying to prove? Is it trying to prove that the German people as a whole were responsible for these events? Or that they were even aware of them? The secrecy of the operation, the geographical location of the camps. The breakdown of

communications in the last days of the war when the extermi-
nations rose into the millions show only too clearly that he is
not stating the truth. The truth is that these brutalities were
brought about by the few extremists. The criminals. Very few
Germans knew what was going on. We did not know! [*It is a
moment before he is able to control his feelings so that he can go on.*]
The most ironic part of it is that the prosecution showed the
films against these defendants. Men who stayed in power for
one reason only—to prevent worse things from happening.
Who is the braver man, the man who escapes in times of peril
or the man who stays at his post at the risk of his own personal safety? [*There is a moment.*] The Defense will present wit-
nesses and letters and documents from religious and political
refugees all over the world telling how Ernst Janning saved
them from execution. The Defense will show the many times
Ernst Janning was able to effect mitigation of sentences when,
without his influence, the result would have been much worse.
We will present affidavits from legal authorities and famed
jurists the world over. The prosecution has in fact presented
only one piece of evidence against Ernst Janning. A notorious
case as the Defense has stated. The Feldenstein case; a case
which never should have been reopened. A case which the
Defense is obliged to review now. The defense calls Mrs. Elsa
Lindnow.

[*Mrs. Elsa Lindnow takes the stand. She is in her early forties.*]

ROLFE: Mrs. Lindnow. What is your occupation?

MRS. LINDNOW: I am a cleaning woman.

ROLFE: Where are you employed?

MRS. LINDNOW: 345 Grossplatz.

ROLFE: Mrs. Lindnow. Did you know Lehman Felden-stein?

MRS. LINDNOW: Yes. I knew him.

ROLFE: In what capacity?

MRS. LINDNOW: He was my employer in 1935.

ROLFE: Do you know the witness, Maria Wallner?

MRS. LINDNOW: Yes.

ROLFE: In what capacity?

MRS. LINDNOW: She was a tenant in the building.

ROLFE: Did you ever see Miss Wallner and Mr. Felden-stein together?

MRS. LINDNOW: Yes.

ROLFE: How did this happen?

MRS. LINDNOW: Mr. Feldenstein came to see Miss Wallner at her apartment.

ROLFE: Often?

MRS. LINDNOW: Quite often.

ROLFE: Mrs. Lindnow. Were there any occasions on which you noticed anything unusual?

MRS. LINDNOW: Yes, I saw Miss Wallner kissing Mr. Feldenstein at the door of her apartment.

ROLFE: Was there any other occasion on which you noticed anything unusual?

MRS. LINDNOW: Yes. There was one.

ROLFE: What was it?

MRS. LINDNOW: I came into Miss Wallner's apartment. I wanted to clean up. I thought it was empty. [Pause.] I saw Miss Wallner sitting on Mr. Feldenstein's lap.

ROLFE: Thank you. The Defense calls Maria Wallner.

[Mrs. Lindnow exits. Maria enters, takes stand.]

ROLFE: Miss Wallner. Did you come here voluntarily? Did you report voluntarily to speak as a witness?

MARIA: Yes.

ROLFE: Is it not true that Colonel Parker asked you to come here? [*Pause.*] Is it not true that it was very disagreeable for you to come here?

MARIA: It is always very disagreeable to live over that time.

ROLFE: That would be in agreement with the information I have that you yourself did not want to come, Miss Wallner. The Nuremberg laws were stated on September 15th 1935. Where were you at that time?

MARIA: In Nuremberg.

ROLFE: Were you aware that physical relationship with Jews was against the law?

MARIA: Yes.

ROLFE: Do you know that in Nuremberg, and Nuremberg in particular, not only a physical relationship with Jews was viewed with disdain, but every social contact?

MARIA: Yes.

ROLFE: Were you aware that it might have some danger for you personally?

MARIA: Yes. I was aware of it. But how could a friendship be discarded from one day to the next because of—

[*Rolfe interrupts. There is even some sensitivity to his voice as he does so.*]

ROLFE: That is another question. I did not ask you that question, Miss Wallner. [*Pause.*] Were you aware of it?

MARIA: Yes. I was aware.

ROLFE: And yet you still continued to see each other?

MARIA: Yes.

ROLFE: Do you remember it was brought out at the trial that Mr. Feldenstein brought you things? Candy and cigarettes?

MARIA: Yes.

ROLFE: Remember that he sometimes brought you flowers?

MARIA: Yes. [*With emotion.*] He brought me things but it was because he was kind. He was the kindest man I ever knew.

ROLFE: Miss Wallner, do you know the witness, Mrs. Elsa Lindnow?

MARIA: Yes. I know her.

ROLFE: Was she a cleaning woman in the apartment you lived in?

MARIA: Yes.

ROLFE: Did Mr. Feldenstein come to see you in your apartment?

[*Pause.*]

MARIA: Yes. He came to see me.

ROLFE: How many times?

MARIA: I don't remember.

ROLFE [*coaxing her*]: Several times?

MARIA: Yes.

ROLFE: Many times?

MARIA: Many times.

ROLFE: Did you kiss him?

[*Pause.*]

MARIA: Yes. I kissed him.

ROLFE: Was there more than one kiss?

[*Pause.*]

MARIA: Yes. [*With emotion.*] But not in the way you are making it sound! He was like a father to me. He was more than my father—

ROLFE: Did you sit on his lap?

COLONEL PARKER [*on his feet*]: Objection, Your Honor. Counsel is persecuting the witness in the pretext of gaining testimony.

NORRIS [*quietly*]: Overruled.

IVES [*quietly*]: Overruled.

HAYWOOD: Objection overruled.

COLONEL PARKER: I cannot accept this ruling, Your Honor.

HAYWOOD [*looks at him quietly*]: I think you'll have to accept it.

COLONEL PARKER: The Defense is being permitted to re-enact what was a travesty of justice in the first place!

HAYWOOD: Colonel Parker. The Tribunal makes the rulings in this case, not the prosecution. [*Then to Rolfe.*] You may continue.

ROLFE: Did you sit on his lap?

MARIA: Yes, but there was nothing wrong or ugly about it.

ROLFE: Did you sit on his lap?

MARIA: Yes.

ROLFE: You sat on his lap. What else did you do?

COLONEL PARKER: Your Honor—

ROLFE: What else do you admit to?

MARIA: Stop it! Stop it!

ROLFE: What else?

[*Janning stands. He speaks almost inaudibly.*]

JANNING: Again?

[*Colonel Parker cannot believe his eyes. Rises.*]

ROLFE [*not seeing him, continues*]: What else?

JANNING: Are you going to do this again?

[*Rolfe wheels and looks at Janning, astounded.*]

ROLFE [*finds a voice somehow*]: Your Honor. The stress the Defendant has been under is so great that he is not aware of . . .

JANNING: I am aware. I am aware.

COLONEL PARKER [*anxiously*]: Your Honor. I believe the defendant wishes to make a statement.

ROLFE: Your Honor. I believe the Defense has a right to request—

HAYWOOD [*bangs gavel*]: Order! Order! [*Turns to Janning.*] Does the Defendant wish to make a statement?

[*Pause.*]

JANNING: Yes. I wish to make a statement.

ROLFE: Your Honor. I believe the Defense has the right to request a recess so that I may speak with my client.

COLONEL PARKER: Your Honor. The Defendant has the right to make his statement now!

HAYWOOD: Tribunal will recess until ten-thirty tomorrow morning.

SCENE: PALACE OF JUSTICE—PRISONERS'
VISITING ROOM

[*Rolfe enters, stares at Janning a moment without speaking.*]

ROLFE: What are you doing? What do you think you're trying to do?! [*Then, with emotion.*] They've had Goering, Frank, Streicher. It's enough!

[*Janning does not respond. Rolfe keeps trying.*]

Do you think I enjoyed being defense counsel during this trial? Do you? There were things I had to do in that courtroom that made me cringe! Why did I do them? Because I want to leave the German people something. I want to leave them a shred of dignity. I want to call a halt to these proceedings! If we allow them to discredit every German like you, we lose the right to rule ourselves forever! [*With emotion rising.*] We have to look at the future. We can't look back. [*Quietly. Indicating guard.*] Do you want the Americans to stay here forever? Do you want that? [*Trying to reach Janning.*] I could show you pictures of Hiroshima and Nagasaki. Thousands and thousands of burnt bodies! Women and children! [*Indicates guard with a thrust of his thumb.*] Is that their superior morality? Where do you think they take us? Do you think they know? Do you think they have any concept of our problems?

[*Janning does not respond.*]

What can I say to you? What can I say to you to make you see?!

JANNING: There is nothing you can say.

SCENE: PALACE OF JUSTICE—COURTROOM

[*Janning sits on the stand.*]

HAYWOOD: Herr Janning, do you wish to make a statement before the Tribunal?

JANNING: I do.

HAYWOOD: Proceed.

JANNING: I wish to testify about the Feldenstein case because it was the most significant trial of the period. It is important not only for the Tribunal to understand it, but the German people. But to understand it, one must understand the period in which it happened. [*He tries to bring the period into words. It is not easy.*] There was a fever over the land. A fever of disgrace, of indignity, of hunger. We had a democracy, yes, but it was torn by elements within. There was, above all, fear. Fear of today, fear of tomorrow, fear of our neighbors, fear of ourselves. [*Pause.*] Only when you understand that can you understand what Hitler meant to us. Because he said to us: "Lift up your heads! Be proud to be German! There are devils among us. Communists, Liberals, Jews, Gypsies! Once the devils will be destroyed, your miseries will be destroyed." It was the old, old story of the sacrificial lamb. [*Seems to look inside himself. The words are hard to come.*] What about us who knew better? We who knew the words were lies and worse than lies? Why did we sit silent? Why did we participate? [*Pause.*] Because we loved our country! What difference does it make if a few political extremists lose their rights? What difference does it make if a few racial minorities lose their rights? It is only a passing phase. It is only a stage we are going through. It will be discarded sooner or later. "The country is in danger." We will "march out of the shadows." "We will go forward." And history tells you how well we succeeded! We succeeded beyond our wildest dreams. The very elements of hate and power about

Hitler that mesmerized Germany, mesmerized the world! [*Remembering with sardonic bitterness.*] We found ourselves with sudden powerful allies. Things that had been denied us as a democracy were open to us now. The world said go ahead, take it! Take Sudetenland, take the Rhineland—remilitarize it— take all of Austria, take it! [*Pause.*] We marched forward, the danger passed. [*Pause; simply.*] And then one day, we looked around and found we were in even more terrible danger. The rites began in this courtroom, swept over our land like a raging, roaring disease! What was going to be a passing phase had become a way of life.

[*There is a moment.*]

Your Honor, I was content to sit silent during this trial. I was even content to let counsel try to save my name. [*As he looks over at Rolfe.*] You have seen him do it. He has done it in this courtroom. He has suggested that the Third Reich worked for the benefit of people. He has suggested that we sterilized men for the welfare of the country. He has suggested that perhaps the old Jew did sleep with the sixteen-year-old girl after all. Once more it is being done out of love of the country. It is not easy to tell the truth. [*With emotion.*] But if there is to be any salvation for Germany those of us who know our guilt must admit it no matter the cost in pain and humiliation. [*Pause.*] I had reached my verdict on the Feldenstein case before I ever came into the courtroom. I would have found him guilty whatever the evidence. It was not a trial at all. It was a sacrificial ritual in which Feldenstein the Jew, was the helpless victim—

ROLFE [*making one last attempt to reach Janning*]: Your Honor, I must interrupt. The Defendant is not aware of what he is saying—he is not aware that—

JANNING: I am aware. I am aware. [*Turns to Haywood.*] My defense counsel would have you believe that we were not aware of concentration camps! [*Pause; cries out.*] Not aware? Where were we?! [*Pause.*] Where were we when Hitler began shrieking his hate in the Reichstag? Where were we when our neighbors were being dragged out of their houses in the middle of the night to Dachau? Where were we when every village in Germany had a railroad terminal where cattle cars were filled with children who were being carried off to their extermination? Where were we when they cried out in the night to us? Were we deaf, dumb and blind?!

ROLFE [*again on his feet*]: Your Honor, I must . . .

JANNING: Maybe we didn't know the details. But if we didn't know, it was because we didn't want to know.

[*Hahn stands up.*]

HAHN: Traitor! Traitor!

HAYWOOD: Order! Order! There will be order! [*Losing his temper.*] Put that man in his seat and keep him there!

JANNING [*looking at Hahn steadily*]: I am going to tell them the truth. I am going to tell the truth if the whole world conspires against it. I am going to tell them the truth about their Ministry of Justice. [*Looks at men in dock.*] Werner Lammpe. An old man who cries into his Bible now. An old man who profited by the property expropriation of every man he sent to the concentration camp. Friedrick Hoffstetter, the good German who knew how to take orders. Who sent men before him to be sterilized like so many digits. Emil Hahn. The decayed, corrupt bigot, obsessed by the devil within himself. [*Finally.*] And Ernst Janning, worse than any of them because he knew what they were and went along with them. Ernst Janning who made his life . . . excrement because he walked with them.

> [*There is a moment. Rolfe rises finally. All eyes in the courtroom are on him. He walks slowly to the stand. He carries, as though by habit, his portfolio with him. He opens the portfolio. He looks down at all the carefully arranged affidavits, arguments. Then he closes the portfolio.*]

ROLFE: Your Honors, it is my duty to defend Ernst Janning. And yet Ernst Janning has said he was guilty. [*Turns to look over at Janning in the dock.*] There is no doubt he feels his guilt. He made a terrible mistake in going along with the Nazi movement, hoping it would be good for his country. But . . . [*Wheels on the judges; says what he has felt for years.*] . . . if he is to be found guilty, there are others who also went along who must also be found guilty. Herr Janning said we succeeded beyond our wildest dreams. Why did we succeed? [*Bends forward.*] What about the rest of the world Your Honors? [*Smiles scathingly.*] Did they not know the intentions of the Third Reich? Did they not hear the words of Hitler broadcast all over the world? Did they not read his intentions in *Mein Kampf*, published in every corner of the world? [*Pause; bends forward.*] Where is the responsibility of the Soviet Union, who in 1939 signed a pact with Hitler and enabled him to make war? Are we now to find Russia guilty? [*Pause.*] Where is the responsibility of the Vatican who signed the Concordat Pact in 1933 with Hitler, giving him his first tremendous prestige? Are we now to find the Vatican guilty? [*Bends forward.*] Where is the responsibility of the world leader, Winston Churchill, who said in an open letter to the *London Times*, in 1938, —1938! Your Honors "Were England to suffer a national disaster, I should pray to God to send a man of the strength of mind and will of an Adolf Hitler." Are we now to find Winston Churchill guilty? [*With special emphasis.*] Where is the responsibility of those American industrialists who helped Hitler to rebuild his arms and profited by that rebuilding? Are we to find the American industrialists guilty? [*Pause.*] No, Your Honor. Germany alone is not guilty. The whole world is as responsible for Hitler as Germany. It is easy to condemn one man in the dock. It is easy to condemn the German people—to speak of the "basic flaw" in German character that allowed Hitler to rise to power—and at the same time, comfortably ignore the "basic flaw" of character that made the Russians sign pacts with him, Winston Churchill praise him, American industrialists profit by him! Ernst Janning says he's guilty. If he is, Ernst Janning's guilt is the world's guilt—no more and no less.

SCENE: GENERAL MERRIN'S OFFICE

[*General Merrin is on phone. Colonel Parker enters.*]

GENERAL MERRIN [*into phone*]: What do you mean they won't let you have it! You can commandeer them! We want every plane that can fly in the air! [*Hangs up; looks at Colonel Parker.*] Tad, just a minute. [*Phone rings. He picks it up.*] Merrin. [*Pause.*] I know there are some of them that don't know the territory. [*Pause.*] I know some of them have never been to Berlin. [*Pause.*] Major, we have to give the Military Governor every help we can give him. We have to get seven hundred tons in the air a day. Seven hundred tons! [*Hangs up. Looks at Colonel Parker. Shakes his head a little.*] This airlift is some operation. We have to get 700 tons of produce to Berlin every day. Did you ever think we would be flying coal and tomatoes in these crates? [*Pause.*] Tad we've always been good friends and that's why I called you in. I want to know what you're going to do in that courtroom tomorrow.

COLONEL PARKER: You know damn well what I'm going to do.

GENERAL MERRIN: Now, here's the problem, Tad. Hitler knew what he was doing when he rehabilitated Germany. He marshaled every important industrialist, politician, military man, judge. You convict these men, you'll make Communism look more attractive to the German people. You'll make them think of us as their persecutors.

COLONEL PARKER: You never cared for these trials, did you, Matt?

GENERAL MERRIN: I wasn't what you call fond of them.

COLONEL PARKER: You never were fond of building an international criminal court, were you?

GENERAL MERRIN: No. And I'll tell you why. We sometimes have to do things for our own security—or, if you will, our own interests—and I personally do not look forward to sitting as a defendant in a trial with those idiots at the U.N. as my prosecutor and judges. If you look at it that way, why not put Truman on trial for dropping the bomb?

COLONEL PARKER: Maybe we should.

GENERAL MERRIN: I'll boil it down to this: We need the help of the German people. And you don't get the support of the German people by giving their leaders stiff prison sentences.

[*It is obvious that General Merrin's words have rocked Colonel Parker.*]

COLONEL PARKER: This is supposed to be a new beginning but it's a new end, isn't it?

GENERAL MERRIN: If you want to be one of those responsible for our losing this struggle with the Soviet Union, think if you're going to be able to live with that. [*Pause.*] Tad, the thing to do is survive, isn't it? Survive as best as we can?

[*Colonel Parker turns and starts. Stops at door.*]

COLONEL PARKER: Just for laughs, Matt. What was the war all about? What was it about?

SCENE: PALACE OF JUSTICE—COURTROOM

[*Colonel Parker reads from documentary evidence. His voice is flat.*]

COLONEL PARKER: Defendant Emil Hahn prepared, signed and circulated reports summarizing NN cases receiving the death penalty at the following special courts on September first, nineteen forty-two: Kiel—two hundred sixty-two defendants from Norway. Essen—eight hundred sixty-three defendants from Belgium and France. Cologne—three hundred thirty-one defendants from France. This concludes the documentary evidence.

[*Puts last document on table before the judges. Looks down at small piece of typewritten paper he has prepared. Then, in a hoarse voice.*]

Your Honors, during the three years that have passed since the end of the war in Europe, mankind has not crossed over the Jordan. Small but terrible wars rage in Greece and Palestine.

And the chorus of international voices is discordant. In our country, the fear of war has been revived and we are constrained once more to look to our defenses. There is talk of "cold war," and meanwhile, men and women die in real wars and the echoes of persecutions and atrocities will not be stilled. These events cannot help but color what happens in the courtroom. [*Pause.*] But somewhere in the midst of these events, the responsibility for the crimes we have brought forward during this case must be placed in true perspective. [*Pause.*] This is the decision that faces Your Honors. It is the dilemma of our times. It is a dilemma that rests with your conscience.

[*Colonel Parker gathers up papers, goes back to prosecution table. Haywood looks at Colonel Parker, stunned that his summation has been so equivocal. Haywood tries to overcome his surprise and goes on.*]

HAYWOOD: The defendants will make their final statements. Frederick Hoffstetter.

HOFFSTETTER [*with the utmost sincerity*]: I have served my country throughout my life and in whatever position I was assigned to, in faithfulness, with a pure heart, and without malice. I followed the concept I believed to be the highest in my profession. The concept that says: "To sacrifice one's own sense of justice to the authoritative legal order. To ask only what the law is and not if it is also unjust." As judge, I could do no other. I believe Your Honors will find me, and millions of Germans like me who believed they were doing their duty to their country to be not guilty.

HAYWOOD: Emil Hahn.

HAHN [*looks at other defendants with contempt*]: I will not say of our policy today that it was wrong when I said yesterday it was right. Germany was fighting for its life! Certain measures were needed to protect it from its enemies. I cannot say I am sorry we applied these measures. We were a bulwark against Bolshevism! We were a pillar of Western Culture! A bulwark the West may yet wish to retain.

HAYWOOD: Werner Lammpe.

LAMMPE: Your Honors . . . [*He tries to make a statement.*] . . . Your Honors . . .

[*The things that have been presented in the courtroom overwhelm him and he finds it impossible to go on. He falls back in his seat, silent.*]

HAYWOOD: Ernst Janning.

JANNING: I have nothing to add to what I have already said.

HAYWOOD: The testimony has been received in the case. Final arguments have been heard. There remains only the task of the Tribunal to render its decision. The record is closed. The Tribunal will recess until further notification.

SCENE: PALACE OF JUSTICE—JUDGES' CHAMBERS

[*Ives and Norris are seated at a table. Ives is reading from a list of documents to Norris. Haywood is standing near a window looking at photographs attached to arrest warrants.*]

IVES: This is the last of the papers of the Night and Fog decree. Do you have any more than that, Ken?

NORRIS: No that's all.

IVES: Now I've collected some precedents here that bear on the basis of the case; the conflict between allegiance to international laws and the laws of one's country. [*To Haywood.*] Dan, we have a mountain of stuff to go over here.

NORRIS: What are you looking at, Dan?

HAYWOOD: I was just looking at the pictures attached to some of the warrants for arrest.

IVES: What pictures?

HAYWOOD: This is a picture of Peterson before they operated on him. [*Puts another indictment on desk.*] Here's a picture of Maria Wallner. She really was sixteen once. Mr. Feldenstein. Case of a boy. Must have been no more than fourteen. Executed for saying that the Reich might lose the war. Authorized by the jurisdiction of Frederick Hoffstetter.

IVES: Now, I think you'll find this more pertinent. This is from the French Chief Prosecutor before the International Military Tribunal: "It is obvious in states organized along modern lines that responsibility is confined to those who act directly for the states since they alone are in a position to judge the legitimacy of the given orders. They alone can and should be prosecuted." I can't see that the prosecution has put forth a really clear-cut case against the defendants.

NORRIS: What about Janning's confession?

IVES: Regardless of the acts committed, I don't see how we can interpret it that the defendants were really responsible for crimes against humanity.

NORRIS: What do you think, Dan?

IVES: Ken, we've been going over these documents for two days. If it isn't clear by now— [*Stops in a burst of frustration and anger.*] Look at these precedents and opinions! Look at them if you're interested at all!

HAYWOOD: I'm interested, Curtiss. You were speaking of crimes against humanity. You were saying these men were not responsible for them. I'd like you to explain that to me.

IVES: I've just been explaining it. I've been explaining it for two days.

HAYWOOD: Maybe. But all I've heard is legalistic double talk and rationalizations. [*Pause.*] Curtiss, when I first became judge I knew there were certain people in the town I wasn't supposed to touch. I knew if I wanted to remain judge, this was so. But how do you expect me to turn my back on millions of murders, how many we don't even really know?

NORRIS: I'm sure he doesn't mean that Dan. There is after all . . .

IVES: I'm not asking you to turn your back on them. I'm asking you what good is it going to do us to pursue this policy?

[*It is a moment before Haywood finally speaks.*]

HAYWOOD: Now we know how those men in the dock felt, don't we?

NORRIS: What do you mean, Dan?

HAYWOOD: They committed murders for the good of their country. Now it's being suggested that we let murderers go free for the good of our country. Isn't that it? [*Pause.*] I'll tell you something, Curtiss. I'm afraid for all of us. How many future genocides will happen unless we draw a line right here?!

IVES: There is a world outside this courtroom. Our country is in danger. That doesn't seem to mean too much to you.

[*Pause.*]

HAYWOOD [*quietly*]: Curtiss. You were saying they weren't responsible. You're going to have to explain it to me. You're going to have to explain it to me very carefully.

SCENE: PALACE OF JUSTICE—COURTROOM

[*Haywood, Norris and Ives walk into the courtroom for the final verdict.*]

CAPT. BYERS: The Tribunal is in session. God save the United States of America and this Honorable Tribunal.

[*Judges take their places.*]

HAYWOOD: The trial conducted before this Tribunal began over six months ago. Simple murders and atrocities do not constitute the gravamen of the charges in the indictment. Rather, the charge is that of conscious participation in a nation-wide government-organized system of cruelty and injustice in violation of legal and moral principles common to all civilized nations. [*Pause.*] The Tribunal has carefully reviewed the record and found therein abundant competent evidence to support, beyond a reasonable doubt, the charges brought against these defendants. Herr Rolfe, in his skillful defense has asserted that there are others who must share the ultimate responsibility for what happened here in Germany. There is truth in this. [*Pause.*] This Tribunal does not believe that the United States or any other country has been blameless of the conditions which made the German people vulnerable to the blandishments and temptations of the rise of Nazism. But this Tribunal does say that the men in the dock are responsible for their acts. The principle of criminal law of every civilized society has this in common. Any person who sways another to commit murder, any person who furnishes the lethal weapon for the purpose of this crime, any person who is an accessory to this crime is guilty. [*Pause.*] Herr Rolfe further asserts that the Defendant Janning was an extraordinary jurist who was acting in what he thought to be the best interests of this country. [*Pause.*] There is truth in this also. [*Looks at Janning.*] Janning, to be sure, is a tragic figure. We believe he loathed the evil he did. But compassion for the present torture of his soul must not beget forgetfulness of the torture and death of millions by the government of which he was a part. Janning's record and his fate illuminate the most shattering truth that has emerged from this trial. If he and the other defendants were all depraved perverts—if all the leaders of the Third Reich were sadistic monsters and maniacs—these events would have no more moral significance than an earthquake or other natural catastrophes. But this trial has shown that under the stress of a national crisis, ordinary men—even able and extraordinary men—can delude themselves into the commission of crimes and atrocities so vast and heinous as to stagger the imagination. No one who has sat through this trial can ever forget. The sterilization of men because of their political beliefs ... The murder of children ... How easily that can happen. There are those in our country today, too, who speak of the protection of the country. Of survival. The answer to that is: survival as what? A country isn't a rock. And it isn't an extension of one's self. It's what it stands for, when standing for something is the most difficult. Before the people of the world—let it now be noted in our decision here that this is what we stand for: justice, truth . . . and the value of a single human being. [*Looks toward Defendants.*] Frederick Hoffstetter—

[*Hoffstetter rises in dock.*]

HAYWOOD: The Tribunal finds you guilty of membership in criminal organizations and crimes against humanity and sentences you to life imprisonment.

[*Hoffstetter looks startled. He had never thought it would come to this.*]

Emil Hahn—

[*Hahn rises in the dock.*]

The Tribunal finds you guilty of war crimes, membership in criminal organizations, and crimes against humanity, and sentences you to life imprisonment.

HAHN: Today you sentence me! Tomorrow the Bolsheviks sentence you!

HAYWOOD: Werner Lammpe—

[*Lammpe rises to his feet slowly with the help of the guard behind him.*]

The Tribunal finds you guilty of membership in criminal

organizations and crimes against humanity, and sentences you to life imprisonment.

[*Lammpe looks about him, tears in his eyes. He sits down slowly.*]

HAYWOOD: Ernst Janning.

[*Janning rises to his feet. He stands erect. Haywood hesitates for the first time before delivering the verdict.*]

Ernst Janning, the Tribunal finds you guilty of crimes against humanity and sentences you to life imprisonment.

IVES: I wish to point out strongly my dissenting vote from the decision of this Tribunal as stated by Justice Haywood, in which Justice Norris concurred. The issues of the actions of the defendants who believe they were acting in the best interests of their country is an issue that cannot be decided in a courtroom alone. It can only be decided objectively in years to come in the true perspective of history.

SCENE: JUDGE HAYWOOD'S QUARTERS

[*Haywood is preparing to leave Nuremberg. Capt. Byers is picking up packed valises. Mrs. Halbestadt enters with cake wrapped in paper. She hands cake to Haywood.*]

MRS. HALBESTADT: Here's something for you to have on the plane.

HAYWOOD: Mrs. Halbestadt, if I take all the food you've given me, we won't have any room to pack anything else.

MRS. HALBESTADT: But it's strudel, Judge! The way you like it.

HAYWOOD: Thank you for everything.

MRS. HALBESTADT: Goodbye, Your Honor.

HAYWOOD: Goodbye. Oh, and give my regards to Mrs. Bertholt. I tried to call her but there wasn't any answer.

MRS. HALBESTADT: Yes, Your Honor. I will.

[*Mrs. Halbestadt exits.*]

HAYWOOD [*to Byers*]: Give my regards to your young lady.

CAPT. BYERS: That's one you owe me.

HAYWOOD: What do you mean?

CAPT. BYERS: Americans aren't very popular in Germany this morning. See you at the airport. [*He exits.*]

[*Haywood understands fully what the impact of the verdict must have been on Mrs. Bertholt. He is suddenly aware of someone standing in the entrance to the study. It is Rolfe.*]

ROLFE: Good afternoon, Your Honor.

HAYWOOD: Good afternoon.

ROLFE: I came here at the request of Ernst Janning. He wishes to see you.

HAYWOOD: I'm just leaving for the airport.

ROLFE: It's on the way. He said it would mean a great deal to him.

HAYWOOD: I'll try.

ROLFE: Thank you. Did you hear about the verdict in the I.G. Farben case, Judge?

[*Haywood does not answer.*]

Most of them were acquitted. The others received light sentences. The verdict came in today.

[*Pause.*]

HAYWOOD: No. I had not heard.

ROLFE: I'll make you a wager.

HAYWOOD: I don't make wagers.

ROLFE: A gentleman's wager. In five years, the men you sentenced to life imprisonment will be free.

[*There is a moment.*]

HAYWOOD: Herr Rolfe. I have admired your work in the courtroom for many months.

[*Rolfe nods politely, accepting the compliment.*]

You are a brilliant attorney. You will undoubtedly go very far. You are particularly brilliant in your use of logic. Therefore I have no doubt that what you suggest may well happen. It is logical in view of the times in which we live. But to be logical is not to be right. And nothing on God's earth could ever make it right.

[*Haywood exits. Rolfe is a little stunned. Somewhere deep within him Haywood's words have reached him. Somewhere within him for a moment he knows that Haywood is right. He knows it. But not for more than a moment, and then he is able to rationalize it away.*]

SCENE: PALACE OF JUSTICE—PRISON CELL

[*Janning sits over notes he has prepared.*]

GUARD: Herr Janning. Someone to see you.

[*Haywood enters. He stares at Janning awkwardly.*]

HAYWOOD: Herr Janning.

JANNING: Judge Haywood. Please. Sit down.

HAYWOOD [*remains standing*]: You wished to see me.

JANNING: Yes. There is something I want to give you. [*Holds out notebook; hands it to Haywood.*] A record of my cases. The ones I remember the details of. I want to give it to someone I can trust.

HAYWOOD [*takes it*]: Thank you. I'll take good care of it.

JANNING: It won't do any good. But it is a record of what can happen. [*Pause.*] Judge Haywood, I know the pressures that must have been brought on you. Your verdict will not be a popular one. You will be criticized greatly. Nuremberg will not be a pleasant word for Germans for years to come. But if it means anything to you, you have the respect of at least one man you convicted. By all that is right in the world, your verdict was a just one.

HAYWOOD: Thank you. What you said in the courtroom— it needed to be said. [*Starts to leave.*]

JANNING: Judge Haywood.

[*The emotion in Janning's voice stops Haywood. Janning goes to him. It's coming, thinks Haywood. Now it comes. The moment he had hoped to avoid.*]

The real reason I asked you to come. I want to know. I want to hear from a man like you. I want to hear—not that he forgives, but that he understands!

[*Haywood stands a moment trying to put it into words.*]

HAYWOOD: I understand the pressures that you faced. No man can say how he would have faced those pressures himself unless he had actually been tested. But how can you expect me to understand sending millions of people to gas ovens?

JANNING: I did not know it would come to that! You must believe it. You must believe it!

[*There is a moment.*]

HAYWOOD [*saying the words as though he were speaking to a child*]: Herr Janning. It came to that the first time you sentenced to death a man you knew to be innocent.

[*Haywood exits. Janning watches him go. Haywood's words come over him in a wave. They have come from the only man in the whole world who could have given him absolution. And that man has laid at his door a greater guilt than he has ever contemplated.*]

CURTAIN

NARRATOR [*in the darkness*]: By April 14, 1949, judgment was rendered in the last of the Nuremberg trials. By 1959, of the ninety-nine sentenced to prison terms only three were still serving their sentences.